The Hardworking Woman's Guide to Money

The Hardworking Woman's Guide to Money

Kathleen Thomas

ISBN: 1977979335
ISBN 13: 9781977979339
Library of Congress Control Number: 2017917018
CreateSpace Independent Publishing Platform
North Charleston, South Carolina

Dedication

To all my sisters and sisters of choice-
Life is a journey, and it means everything to me to walk it with you.

HE ———
G WOMAN'S
MONEY

E E N
I A S

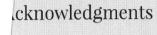

mas
535
ters.com

ation visit

ers.com

Acknowledgments

I would like to thank the following people who helped me make this book possible:

My mom who taught me that if I worked hard, I could achieve what I wanted, and to my husband who has always been my biggest cheerleader.

Jack Fehr and Jaclyn Fitzgerald who helped me find and develop my voice as a writer.

Everyone who encouraged me along the way to follow my dreams, even if they were a little scary.

A YOUNG WOMAN PAYING

ough college. Or maybe yo
ho always relied on your
financial decisions. In an
ging your own finances ca
orating, intimidating, and
frightening.

ess of your stage in life, th
ovide the information you
e confident, informed fina
ions. Author Kathleen Th
ncise, empathetic guide co

mportance of establishing
it,
account charges and fees
tgages,
ege costs and payment opt
ployee benefits,
estments,
ate planning,
irement income,
d more.

ing charge of your financi
of the wisest moves you'll
and with Thomas as your g
soon be a master money m

Kathleen Thom
Financial Planne
often goes by K T
the financial serv
over two decac
founder of NewD
independent reg
fir

ISBN 978-1-9779-793

9 781977 979793

Foreword

*T*he *Hardworking Woman's Guide to Money* is designed to help you build on the personal finance knowledge you already possess to develop a stronger, saner approach to your financial goals.

You already know you need to save for retirement, but you may not know how to do it most efficiently. You know the importance of your employee benefits, but it's easier to renew the same ones each year than to check your alternatives.

You might even be aware of the pink tax and the red purse. The pink tax is when a woman pays more for a product, such as $1 more for your unscented deodorant, than a man pays for the exact same product. The red purse, as you may know, signifies the financial inequity facing working women.

You only have so many hours in the day, so you do your best to juggle all of life's financial tasks while also managing home, family, and career, not to mention dealing with the pink tax and red purse.

Let me suggest one way to fight back: Find another 1% of income to put away for retirement. How, you ask? Look for ways to cut corners. Consider buying the cheaper deodorant, or decide that you will do take out once a week instead of twice a week. But maybe you like to treat yourself. That's OK too, if you can learn to change your mind-set about what treating yourself really means. Would you rather buy yourself an expensive weekend away for your birthday each year or cut corners throughout the year and gift yourself a 1% annual increase in retirement savings?

You can also fight back by taking time to read through your work place benefits information. Save money by trimming what you really don't need and buying what you do. Understand that after healthcare, disability income insurance may be the benefit you need most. After all, your income is one of your biggest assets.

I'll tell you where it's worth paying more attention. You might have heard about Wells Fargo signing up unaware customers for additional services. Customers might have been aware of the services they opted into had they read the fine print. Taking a few extra minutes can help you understand money wasters hidden in fine print, from high overdraft charges to the real costs of cable television and cell phone service.

You can take control of these and other financial areas. I've seen it done many times before—hardworking women overcoming obstacles to achieve multiple financial challenges. You can learn through trial and error, or avoid common mistakes by becoming a willing student.

Dust yourself off, become willing to learn, and start walking down the right financial path. You can do this by understanding basic financial concepts and how emotions influence our money decisions. I often tell my clients that it's hard to get over who you are and move past your fears. The decisions some of us make are driven by our fears, like going broke. Financial insecurity can be a burden, but it can also help you accomplish hard goals like buying a home or paying off your mortgage before you retire. My mom showed me this lesson when her fear of losing the home provided by my father's employer drove her to save for a new family home.

My mom was a stay-at-home mother, a child of immigrants who struggled financially like many others during the Great Depression. My dad had a job that came with a house, but she was always afraid he would lose his job and we would become homeless. It didn't matter that my father was well liked and often promoted at his job. Her fear was an inside job. Each week, she took $5 from her household allowance and put it into a "house" account. She was relentless in pursuit of this goal.

It took 10 years of passbook savings (Mom's house account), an eventual job outside of our home, and negotiations with a homebuilder before she could come up with 20% down on a modest new house. This was a feat I grew to appreciate as I made my own way financially.

I'd like to say Mom's monumentally disciplined effort steered me on my own road to financial success, but alas, I proved the adage that you also learn from your own mistakes. Sum up my financial mistakes with this one phrase: I didn't establish my own, separate financial identity. It's something many women neglect even today. Chalk it up to emotions, to understandable optimism.

Some 25 years ago, as my career began to flourish, my first marriage floundered. We had joint bank accounts and joint credit. Every newlywed thinks their marriage will last forever, so why not?

Then we suddenly separated. He went one way with our "joint" money and credit, while I went the other way with my credit rating badly damaged.

That's when I decided to take a chance on myself. I divorced and found the career I still love today. It wasn't easy. There weren't many female financial advisors back then, and there was not much of a safety net as I became self-employed almost immediately. Today, women are the majority of new business owners. They want more control and appropriate pay. We're not there yet, but we're working at it. And we're taking risks to make it happen.

Consequently, I couldn't believe anything more strongly than the fact women need our own separate financial identities. Maybe you're happily married, as I've been for the last 19 years. Maybe most of your assets are jointly owned. No matter how promising your union, establish a separate financial identity.

Establish your own credit, because statistics show that with longer lives and high divorce rates, you will probably need it at some point in your life.

Establishing good individual credit is just one habit hardworking women need. My goal is to help you better understand life's other financial puzzles, knowing that there is little time in today's busy world. I'll help you address life's trade-offs. Work less or more? Save for retirement or a child's college tuition? These questions puzzle many Americans, but women suffer more severe consequences when they don't solve their unique financial puzzles.

I have seen firsthand what happens when women don't own their financial lives. I found what studies now regularly show: Women are consultative and want a relationship they can trust. I learned this when I started out working with widows who discovered their financial situation for the first time. I continue to learn from hardworking women, both sophisticated and less so in financial matters. I learned from and earned the trust of women because I understand that money is a not an end, but a means to an end.

I hope to earn your trust in the following pages. Perhaps you won't count your first million upon finishing this book, but my hope is that you will better understand your financial challenges and gather strategies that will help you work toward solutions.

Read this book cover to cover, or focus on specific topics. If you need information in a pinch, the quick guides at the end of each chapter could help. Each of these offers easy-to-digest morsels that can help you through life's various financial challenges.

Then, examine your own financial life, think about your dreams and goals, and continue to build toward your financial goals. It's hard, but we're used to a challenge. We're women.

One

The 7 Habits of Financially Successful, Hardworking Women

How does a hardworking woman become a financially savvy woman? How does she get ahead when it comes to money?

If you're like most hardworking women I know, you race from one task to the next, often running ingloriously to your next task while still completing the previous one. That's not the image I remember from the 70s, which promoted perfume by singing a jingle about a woman who could do it all.

Do you remember this: "I can bring home the bacon...fry it up in a pan...and never, ever let you forget you're a man"? Then the voiceover talks about an "eight-hour perfume for the 24-hour woman."

Yeah, right!

Many women I know scold themselves endlessly about the things they fail to do. No matter what they complete, they focus on what needs to be done—like a growing to-do list. Perfume isn't going to help.

If you fit this description, stop beating yourself up. Instead, find the resources you need to handle your finances more efficiently. I hope I can help. The following seven habits, I believe, can help every hardworking woman cut through the noise and hype to better manage her time and resources.

1. **Understand your situation.** Where are you in your life right now? Where do you want to go? It's your story, your life.

   Whether building or rebuilding your separate financial identity, maintaining a successful financial regimen, or building on family wealth, you need a starting point to measure the distance between now and future financial success.

2. **Be willing to learn.** You don't need advanced financial degrees to understand your financial situation, but you should be a willing student. Learn the basics. For example, understand your bank charges and credit card rates. Know how companies derive your credit score—and how to improve it.

   Prepare yourself before—not after—buying any financial product or service. Ask the critical questions needed to help you fully understand your credit, mortgages, and bank products, which are often complex, although they are marketed as simple.

   Also understand the time value of money. You know the earlier you save, the better your financial future will look. If you start saving late for a goal, you can always catch up, but saving early is a proven financial habit worth its weight in gold. Saving early and regularly is a financially savvy habit possessed by hardworking women. You'll find that time matters—it really does.

3. **Establish guideposts.** Women increasingly occupy and excel in the halls of corporate and government power. Some studies show that female-run corporations outperform companies led by men, which doesn't surprise me. In a male-dominated field like finance, I've had my own opportunity to see how I could use my skills to excel in my industry. Clients tell me that they like the fact that I talk "English" to them and not jargon. They also like the fact that I can engage people of both sexes. I wasn't aware that this skill was so unique, but apparently women are better communicators in general. Women are also increasingly taking financial matters into their own hands, but not always with the same confidence they exhibit in the workplace. Maybe it's because of inflexible financial

rules some financial gurus—I call them the "budget police"—demand we follow. You needn't engrave a budget in stone.

My alternative? Guideposts. They require you to pay attention to the big picture. How much does your life cost, and how will that change over time? We're estimating here, just as you can estimate a time frame for retirement or a college fund for a child. Even without a budget, you innately understand where each item you buy fits into your financial picture.

Guideposts should take into account the items you *must have*, those you *don't really need*, and those you *don't need at all*. You instinctively know that you don't really need to spend money on three restaurant dinners a week or on a new car because you just paid the loan on your current auto. Guideposts are about the common sense that tells you the car loan payment you don't make anymore would fit nicely into your company 401(k) plan or a child's college savings account.

4. **Take charge.** In an environment where an assertive woman is often called a bitch, I'm here to tell you there is nothing wrong with being an informed, in-control woman. Nothing!

We often don't question our worth in the workplace. We don't question pricing, like asking how one company's car insurance can save you 15%. Compared to what? We don't ask how a financial advisor makes money either. Hardworking women who become financially savvy learn how to unapologetically ask the tough questions.

Asking the tough questions will make you a Doubting Thomas, a person who knows truth from fiction. You're negotiating for a new car price, and the salesperson tells you the manager gave a final offer. Hogwash. Threaten to leave. Or pull out numbers from a buyer's service, like *Consumers Digest*, to let everyone know that *you know* the true costs.

Learn to negotiate. A Doubting Thomas negotiates to get the right product at the right price. A Doubting Thomas is paid what she is worth, but is also willing to say "no" to herself and others. She knows a discount is only meaningful if she was going to buy a product or service anyway. Buying something at 50% off regular price is still more expensive than not buying it at all—a 100% off sale.

Remember, you *need something, don't really need it,* or *don't need it at all.* Most purchases should fall into the first category, a few might fall into the second, and you don't need anything that falls into the third.

The more you challenge the status quo, the more natural being a Doubting Thomas will feel.

5. **Embrace change.** Women know change is constant. Tax rates and deductions change over time. You need this much insurance now and that much later. You can take more investment risk early in your life, but you need more stability as you near financial goals. The list goes on.

Hardworking women who are financially savvy embrace this change. They nimbly change financial circumstances when required. You can do this, too. Plan to meet your needs, knowing they will morph with your financial readiness and the stages of your life.

Understand that life throws us curveballs in the form of layoffs and disability that can interrupt and even damage our long-range plans. Be ready for anything, and you'll react more favorably to changing financial circumstances as they happen.

6. **Use the right resources at the right time.** Hardworking women who are financially savvy know that as they travel through life and experience different stages, their finances will change accordingly. They learn about and use the financial tools appropriate for each stage.

Maybe the right resources for a younger person are employee benefits and a company 401(k). Or the right resource for a first-time homebuyer might be a buyer's real estate agent. The beginning investor might turn to an online advisor to help with simple investments.

You grow older and things change. Now, you might need an accountant for your taxes and a registered investment advisor for more complex finances. Perhaps you'll need to find a qualified professional who can talk to you about disability income insurance, life insurance, and long-term care insurance. You may even need professional guidance in the form of a real, live advisor.

A financially savvy woman buys some insurance through her employer and supplements it on her own if needed. This is great starting point. Learn as much as possible about your benefits. Then maybe you max out your retirement plan at work and invest more through individual resources, because you understand that longer lives create different financial needs for women.

7. **Pay attention to income planning.** Financially savvy women often find an advisor, a partner, who can help them stretch out their retirement money to prepare for retirement. We call it income planning, and we help people take income from their investments, retirement accounts, and even Social Security and try to make it last. Income planning is as important as saving for retirement, but it can be more complex.

Do you take taxable income first and let tax-deferred investments continue to grow? How do you pass assets on to a loved one or charity? Do you transition or dive headfirst into retirement?

People who figure out how to retire with some predictable income and without a mortgage and other debt don't worry about money like people who didn't plan for retirement. Their solutions may be simpler than you think.

Let's look at one example you might not think of as income planning: paying off your mortgage. Many financial experts suggest paying an extra mortgage payment per year to help reduce the time it takes to pay in full. They're right. But what if your monthly mortgage payment is $2,400? This sounds to many like a tough nut to crack. It isn't.

If you're not in a financial position to make an entire extra mortgage payment one month each year, try this: Divide your $2,400 monthly mortgage payment by 12 months, and you get $200 per month. Finding $200 extra per month is easier than finding 12 times that amount per month. Two roads, but the same results.

I've identified these and other habits that help people become financially successful. Every person possesses the ability to use these actions for his or her greater financial good, but it depends on willingness, discipline, awareness, and other human traits you already possess. When you understand how to develop these habits and you break through your psychological barriers to take appropriate action, your financial prospects will benefit.

Hardworking women who are also financially savvy aren't smarter than the rest of us. They're willing and able learners. We'll dig deeper into each of the following characteristics on our journey together, but here's a sneak preview. To become a financially savvy consumer, you should understand your unique situation.

Quick Guide 1: How to Strengthen Your Financial Identity

Your financial identity means everything when it comes to meeting your financial goals. Establishing a good credit history can keep your cost of borrowing low, giving you more money to put toward long-range goals, such as buying a first home or preparing for retirement.

I talk to hardworking women all the time about the importance of building and strengthening their own credit histories separate from their spouses. All too often, I see women, middle-aged and older, who are emotionally and financially devastated by divorce or the death of a loved one. They are left without a financial clue or stitch of credit because they never established their own financial identities.

Here's how you can establish (or reestablish) and strengthen your own financial identity.

TO DO

1. **Get a copy of your credit report.** Your joint credit history counts, but not as much as having your own. Go to www.annualcreditre-port.com to get a free credit report once a year or any time you are denied credit. The report consolidates your credit history from all 3 credit bureaus: Equifax, Experian, and Transunion. Be prepared to give your name, address, Social Security number, and date of birth to get a report.

2. **Check your credit report thoroughly.** Look for money you didn't know you owed, errors, and other negative marks, such as a high debt-to-available-credit ratio.

3. **Pay your bills on time.** Doing this obsessively is the biggest single habit you can develop to build your own good credit history. If you're beyond busy, automate your bill paying with your bank.

4. **Consider getting an annual FICO score.** Get a free estimate from www.myfico.com, one or more of the 3 credit bureaus, or even some credit cards. Scores range from 350 to 800, with

higher meaning better. Check your score periodically to monitor changes.

5. **Start over if needed.** Even with a bad credit history, you can qualify for bank accounts and find credit cards that you prefund. Then work your way up from there.

Quick Guide 2: How to Figure Your Net Worth

While you may not care much about your net worth during your working years, it could play an outsized role in how financially comfortable you are in retirement. The next section shows you how to figure out your net worth.

STEPS

1. **List all your assets.** This includes everything, both liquid and illiquid. Make a chart like this:

Table 1. Assets list.

Liquid assets	Illiquid assets	Something in between
Cash		Annuities
Checking/savings account	Master Limited Partnerships	Bank account with minimum balance
Many stocks	Real estate	Certain stocks
Many bonds	Collectibles	Certain bonds
Most mutual fund shares	Your privately held business	Certain mutual fund shares
Retirement account assets upon reaching retirement age		Retirement account assets before reaching retirement age
CDs reaching maturity		CDs not reaching maturity
Life insurance policy cash value		

2. **Value your assets.** Loosely calculate the value of your home and car on a variety of online sites. Consult valuation experts to learn how much collectibles or a family business are worth.

3. **List all your liabilities.** List all your debt, including mortgages, credit card balances, and car loans. Don't forget about cosigned loans. They count, too.

4. **Assets - liabilities = net worth.** Total your assets, liquid and il-liquid, and subtract your total liabilities—your debt—to come up with your net worth.

5. **Stay current.** Rinse and repeat every few years as goals and your net worth change.

ONE CAVEAT

You should calculate a real market price for most items, but some are worth more to you in sentimental value than to anyone else looking solely at market value. Know the difference.

Two

Habit 1: Understand Your Situation

I escaped a banking job and launched my own financial planning business in the early 1990s. I realized that if I wanted to get paid what I was worth, I needed to pay myself. That's basically what financial advisors do. During this time, I became involved in the local Business and Professional Women's Foundation (BPW). My BPW chapter was filled with many women with the same struggles, all trying to advance professionally. I attended the 1995 BPW national conference in Washington, DC. Election campaigns were in full swing, and the "woman vote" mattered. We heard both incumbent president Bill Clinton and his challenger, Bob Dole, speak.

First, Bob Dole. The president of BPW gave him a red purse. He said, "Thanks! Elizabeth will love it!"

Next, Bill Clinton, who, when offered the red purse, held it up and said, "Let's turn this red purse black!" He got it. We have made a lot of progress since then, but there is still widespread financial disparity in many professions.

My desire for this book is to offer women advice and encouragement they can use to untangle their finances. I want every woman's red purse to turn black, but we are not a homogeneous group. This doesn't mean we don't share common challenges. We are behind when it comes to financial security, and we are more likely to serve as caregivers for children and elderly parents.

We also live longer. A female born in 1970 was expected, on average, to live 74.7 years, according to the Centers for Disease Control and Prevention. That's some seven years longer than males born the same year. A female born in 2014 is expected to live, on average, 81 years. Interestingly, the longevity gap between genders closes to about five years for people born in 2014.

The older you are, the longer you'll live. Women reaching age 65 in 2015 are expected to live an additional 21.6 years, compared to 19.3 additional years for men of the same age.

Clearly, women must finance retirement longer than men do. We know women have multiple sources of stress as they age. 7 in 10 women ages 65 and older live alone, and those who live alone are more likely to experience financial stress, according to Pew Research. I always joke with my girlfriends that if we all find ourselves widowed, we could live together. Living alone in retirement can be both lonely and expensive. Many of my widowed clients live alone. In a lot of ways, our society isolates widows in the former marital home. There has been some shift in this with younger widows who are often still working and making their way in life. But older widows who are at or past retirement age, like my mom, are far more common, so they need to have additional resources.

Women make up 53–68% of caregivers for sick and disabled relatives, according to different estimates. The AARP Public Policy Institute says that in the United States are women—that's about 25 million women! I have many clients trying to take care of both their children and parents at the same time. We call these folks the sandwich generation, as they are wedged between caring for both older and younger loved ones. For the most part, these caregivers are women.

Whatever the exact number of women caregivers, we know they suffer financial consequences in return for their caregiving. The MetLife Mature Market Institute found that female caregivers lost an average of $324,044 in wages and Social Security benefits over their lifetimes. That is a pretty significant amount to try to live without, but by the time you are needed as a caregiver, caring for a loved one is not a choice but an obligation.

It's not all bad news. Other statistics show the financial outlook for women is improving. We've heard forever that half of all marriages end in divorce, but that's not really the case. The divorce rate could be in the 30–40 range, according to the *New York Times*. Of course, falling divorce rates do not mean a thing to those who do divorce and suffer financially because of it.

Women are also making gains in the equal pay battle, with the US Department of Labor's Bureau of Labor Statistics reporting that women earn, on average, $719 per week, or 83 percent of what men make. While leaving plenty of room for improvement, these numbers are more promising than past statistics. For example, when I entered the professional work force in 1985, the gap was closer to 70%. Employers didn't seem to take women seriously at that time. I remember when my first professional boss took me out for dinner to talk with me about the future. What he really wanted to ask me—but didn't dare ask at the office—was whether I was planning a family that might be in the way of his business plan. The crazy thing was that this didn't seem an unreasonable question in 1985.

All of the issues outlined above also affect the amount women receive on average from Social Security, where the average benefit for men is $16,590 annually, while women receive $12,587.

One reason is that Social Security bases recipients' benefits on lifetime earnings, so it's not surprising that 11.6% percent of women age 65 and older live in poverty, according to a report by the U.S. Department of Commerce.

There are tons of other statistics about the demise of traditional retirement plans, the inadequacy of 401(k)-type plans, how women invest compared to men, and the readiness of women—and men—to be on the receiving end of the greatest wealth transfer in American history.

Yet, hardworking women find ways to make advances.

Those who plan everything to the final detail might choose to have children later rather than earlier. Researchers from Washington University in Missouri found that women in Denmark who had children at age 30 or younger earned less than those who waited to have their first child after that age. I have seen more than a few of my clients intentionally establish a career before a family. This choice can open up real opportunities to grow income and experience that will lead to more options after starting a family.

With today's workforce being more mobile than ever, many professionals get the option to work from home some or all of the time. This can be an ideal solution for a mom returning to work; however, those who get these offers are typically more independent workers, and the privilege of working from home usually comes with tenure. The work-from-home trade-off can give working women better options to manage their time when they are working and raising a family.

Here's another fun fact: 20 women were chief executive officers of Standard & Poor's 500 companies in May 2016. That is only 4%, which doesn't seem hopeful for hardworking women trying to climb their way to the top, but it wasn't that long ago that there were no female CEOs of large companies. Women are *slowly* making their way to the executive suites, cracking—if not yet breaking—the glass ceiling. We also must remember that, as a nation, we have still been unable to elect a female leader to the White House. Whether you were for or against Hillary Clinton as president, she did a lot to drive forward the idea of a female president. Someday, you will be able to say to your girls that they can become anything that they want, just like their brothers, but we aren't there yet.

Statistics are interesting, but let's talk about individuals. I have seen women executives who are supremely confident in everything they do in their careers but do not have nearly the same confidence when it comes to managing their money.

To these and other women, I offer perhaps my most important piece of advice in the title of the next section.

KNOWLEDGE EQUALS POWER

Know that you probably can't have it all if you want to have children and, heaven forbid, spend a little time raising them. As a potential parent, you need to decide what's important right now. Some families have one spouse making enough money that the other can stay home, but in the last 30 years, life has become far more expensive than when your mother perhaps made the decision, so a single-income family is not always financially feasible.

When you start or grow a family, you need to figure out just how much income will come in, what expenses you can eliminate, and how long can you afford to be out of work. This is where the power of planning really excites me. Some of my clients want to get right back into the workforce and keep climbing. They want the ability to provide their children with a lifestyle they couldn't afford without returning to work. Some have exciting careers that they want to pursue, but they want to spend a good deal of time at home before returning to work. And others desire to be stay-at-home parents but simply cannot afford it. Remember that the only right choice is the one that best suits the needs of your family—financially and otherwise. The mom shaming needs to come to an end. Every woman has different personal and familial goals, and that's OK. Besides, we never judge a man for going right back to work or socializing after the birth of a child, so we women need to stop judging one another for the choices that make the most sense given our unique circumstances.

We make these choices every day. Learn about money as you would learn about anything that can advance your career. Financial advisors take certification courses. Business executives study for advanced degrees. Why shouldn't financial consumers—that's all of us—learn more about money?

Now you might think, "Look at her. She's a financial advisor. That's easy for her to say."

OK, maybe it is easy for me now. But I learned the hard way. I told you a little about how my first marriage ended in an emptied bank account and maxed-out credit cards. I also told you about my mother saving $5 a week, which was my first personal finance lesson. I didn't tell you about my second lesson, learned when I was an 18-year-old college freshman.

My first experience with a checking account taught me that the balance you see when you check it isn't always the balance available. I bounced a $5 check at the college bookstore and paid a $25 penalty for the miscue. This stung, because needless to say, if I could have afforded the $25 penalty, the $5 check never would have bounced. This is an example of "not knowing what you don't know," but it happens all the time to consumers. When something seems so simple, we often forget to pay attention to it only to wind up making a mistake that costs us.

Checking accounts with Visa debit cards have gotten more than a few people in trouble, as they are unsure what part is actual cash and what part is borrowed cash. A bit more complicated are loans and credit cards. When savings accounts today pay only one-quarter of 1%, why would you carry a balance on a credit card that charges 19% interest? Why even own such a card when it is a disaster waiting to happen? I would empty my savings account that paid hardly any interest and put all the cash toward my high-interest-rate credit card, because 19% is a lot (I'll show you just how much in quick guide 4 at the end of chapter 2).

We make mistakes like keeping balances on high-interest cards, because nobody teaches us about money. We don't know who to go to for advice, because money is the last taboo subject. People will talk about their sex lives before they broach the subject of money. This has to change.

Talking about your salary, the price of your house, or the cost of your car isn't talking about money; it's bragging. Assessing your retirement investments, learning how (and why) to pay an affordable amount for your mortgage, learning how to invest throughout your lifetime—now that's talking about money.

We can't be afraid to ask questions about money. We must understand that as financial consumers, we make common mistakes and have similar misunderstandings. You, I, and women everywhere can change the equation by learning more, by becoming willing students.

IT'S YOUR FINANCIAL JOURNEY

If I've been successful, I've piqued your interest and you'll want to learn more. Yes, the challenges are many, but I believe solutions exist for most financial obstacles. Now is as good a time as any to start.

We are in the throes of the greatest transfer of wealth in history. Some $16 trillion will change hands globally over the next three decades, according to Wealth-X and NFP Family Wealth Transfers Report. Some of those hands might belong to you. What will you do with that money, whether it's a large or small sum? Will you know how to manage it, or will it manage you?

Even if you're not in on the great wealth transfer, learn how baby steps can help you take great strides toward meeting wealth accumulation goals for a first home, college tuition, retirement, and to leave loved ones or charities a financial legacy. Remember, my mom turned $5 a week into almost $20,000.

Do *something*. If you truly can't put away 10% of your income for retirement, save less. Save something!

Now that you understand how you might fit—or not fit—in with statistics I've cited here, understand how you can vault the institutional barriers facing you. *You* are in the best position to understand *your* personal financial health.

Think of any financial challenge as a road trip. Your trip might be a short hop to buy groceries or a longer jaunt to visit friends. Each trip requires you to understand your starting point, finish line, and a course of action to take you from here to there. Each trip requires you to *do something*, to understand your situation. A plane will make your 500-mile trip faster, but maybe driving gets you there more cheaply. Either way, you're doing something. The only way you won't finish is if you don't start the trip.

My philosophy when it comes to finances is *something is always better than nothing*.

Doing nothing ultimately is a decision to do something. Understand your situation, and be willing to learn how to make your financial trip better.

Quick Guide #3: The Time Value of Money

The time value of money is based on the simple premise that in the future, your money will be worth more than it is today.

Think about it. Lawyers cobble together agreements that spread financial settlements over many years. State lottery commissions pay out grand prizes over 20–30 years. There's a reason for that: the time value of money. Look at the following example to see how time can swell your savings:

Let's say Jessica puts $100 a month away every year for 40 years. That's $48,000 total—impressive even without having earned a dime on the amount. Now look at what she would accumulate if her money earned just 5% annually—less than what stocks have earned on average over time. After 40 years and a moderately low annual return, Jessica amassed $152,602. Impressive, right?

Saving early and regularly is a financially savvy habit, an action you take. Doing nothing is also an action, one that will hurt more than you might think later in life. This is the cost of procrastination:

Melissa doesn't save a dime for 20 years, but she thinks she can make up for lost time. So, instead of putting away $100 per month, she doubles it to $200. This will bring her to the same total contribution—$48,000—after 20 years that Jessica will have after 40 years. But her money won't grow over 20 years like Jessica's will over 40 years. Using the same 5% annual interest rate, Melissa can only grow her money to $82,206. Let's break down this example:

Table 2. Savings comparison

	Monthly contribution	Number of years saving	Total contributions	Total accumulated at 5% interest
Jessica	$100	40	$48,000	$152,602
Melissa	$200	20	$48,000	$82,206

What happened? Procrastination hurt. Compound interest had more time to work its magic in the first example because it was combined with more time. That's the time value of money. Your money, especially when you reinvest earnings, always grows fastest in later years. The earlier you begin saving, the better your eventual result will be.

TIME VALUE OF MONEY IN REVERSE

Remember earlier in chapter 2 when I talked about a credit card charging 19% interest? A person with little credit history or one including missed payments might pay that much for the use of a credit card.

Minimum payments can hurt you too! Many credit cards show how many years it would take to pay off a credit card if you only make the minimum payments, and they often show 20 years plus!

When I see this on my statement, I think to myself, no way I'll be wearing that new sweater for 20 years!

That's why you can typically save more money by paying off high-interest credit cards than by investing the same money. Think about it. Few investments earn 19% annually.

Time matters. It really does.

Quick Guide 4: 7 Ways to Establish a Strong Financial Foundation

Chapter 2 outlines many of the reasons why women should establish a strong financial foundation. Consider these 7 tips to get started.

1. **Establish your own financial identity.** Establish your own financial identity by having credit cards and checking and savings accounts in your name.

2. **Engage in all family money decisions.** In every family, there is the division of jobs. Often, I see one spouse handling the shopping and one handling the yardwork. Although the divide-and-conquer strategy works when it comes to running the family, adding money to the situation can throw off the balance of power in the family. If you share your life with someone, make sure not to just turn it over. Most fights between couples are about spending decisions. If you are choosing to be the unengaged partner in when it comes to financial decisions, you have also given up your voice in the finances.

3. **Become involved in investing decisions.** I cannot tell you how many times I have heard people I work with say, "The financial professional I am working with only talks to my husband. It's like I'm not even in the room." If you have hired a professional, whether a financial advisor, CPA, or lawyer, and he or she only listens to one spouse, it's time to look for a new professional.

4. **Use time to your advantage.** Begin saving as soon as you can, no matter how small the amount, and increase your savings amount at least once annually.

5. **Understand the enormity of tomorrow.** By now, we get it. We will likely live longer and need more income. Make sure you can afford your spending plan in retirement, or you will become the one left holding the empty bag.

6. **Make personal money decisions wisely.** I tell my clients never to lend family or friends any money they can't afford to lose. That's because lending to those closest to us is a volatile recipe for financial and family pain. What happens if repayment never comes? If you loaned your retirement money, it will hurt much more than lending disposable income.

7. **Shop with a purpose.** Did you ever go to a department store determined to buy one or two things, only to see the latest "sale of the century" swell your shopping list? You're not alone. Become a discerning shopper, the kind who doesn't buy things she doesn't need. The sale of the century will happen again...and again...and again.

Three

Habit 2: Be Willing to Learn

Have you ever wondered how companies selling products and services can afford to offer you 0% financing? How about rebates on cars or a free upgrade for a mobile phone contract? My favorite of these freebies—and those who know me well have heard this before—is the free GPS we get from satellites. GPS is one of the most helpful tools, and yet it's free. And why would you want to pay for it if it's free? Think about it. Your GPS always offers you at least two routes but recommends the one that takes you by the most stores. A valuable commodity that you get for free always has a catch. To find out what the catch is, you must become a financial detective and launch an investigation. In the case of the GPS, the catch is that it steers you toward stores—many of which display advertisements when you're stopped at red light—and encourages you to shop at places you might not otherwise consider had your GPS not taken you by them.

Let's apply the same detective skills to your finances. Credit card companies know that a large percentage of well-intentioned consumers will not pay the balance off before the end of the free interest period, but what most of us don't know is that if you owe even $5 at the end, you will pay all the interest due from day one at their published rate of 14%–29%. That's the catch.

This is so profitable that free interest offers are everywhere. Free financing is rarely used to pay down our debt, because it's tempting to use your available credit on items you cannot typically afford as well as items you might not choose to buy if you had to part with the cold, hard cash.

Paying for these unnecessary items with credit doesn't mean you don't have to pay for them. Before you use that free-interest credit card, ask yourself, "If I had to take the funds from my savings account to buy this item, would I still make the purchase?" If the answer is no, you might want to slow down and apply the 24-hour rule.

What's the 24-hour rule, you ask? It's simple. Before you make a frivolous purchase, give yourself a day, and then ask yourself if you still think the purchase makes sense given your other competing plans for those funds. There is a lot of pressure in the showroom of a car dealer and easy free financing at the furniture store, but you are in charge. You can leave or tell them you will decide tomorrow.

So, why don't we?

A FALSE CONFIDENCE

There are many studies about decision making and what gets in the way of learning what we need to know before making major decisions. The trend of deciding without learning costs Americans untold millions every year. I see it play out consistently: car leasing or buying, stock picking, finance decisions, benefits selections at work, and home buying at speeds that the distracted human mind cannot process at successfully.

There are fundamentally two factors at play when trying to make quick money decisions, or, for that matter, most decisions.

First, is an oversized sense of confidence that we know what we are doing, even if we don't. The information age, for all of its advantages, has created a sound bite or quick phone check for information that is accepted as fact and repeated over and over again. Gone are the days when we spent time fact-checking our information.

Second is the fear that others will think that we cannot make a decision or that we don't have the brains to figure it out. People actually feel pressured into decisions that they wanted time to think over and make decisions they often regret because they feel others will judge them if they are unable to make a quick decision.

I believe if you are reading this book, you are trying to work your way past these hurdles, so I have some ideas that might help.

HOW TO LEARN

Tools of convenience may be a good place to start, but there is a lot of misinformation out there.

Just because you find information on Facebook or Twitter doesn't make it true. Just because Siri gives you an answer doesn't make it the solution that's right for you.

So, first, consider the source. Does the person trying to influence your decision have a personal reason—like receiving a commission off your purchase—for encouraging you to make a hasty decision? If so, apply the 24-hour rule.

When someone slides you a contract to sign and says, "Initial, initial, and sign," take the contract in your hand, set down the pen, and read it rather than blindly signing it. If they seem to be rushing to finish it, offer to take it home to read. That usually slows them right down.

If you are headed to a big box store, say Home Depot, Lowes, a furniture store, or a car dealership, make a plan before you go. What are you there to look at? Are you buying today or doing research today?

If you have a spouse or partner, make a pact about the plan, and tell the salesperson right away that your plan is *not* to buy today.

If you are headed out holiday shopping, keep yourself on track by making a list of who you are buying for and the amount you hope to not exceed in the purchase. It's also helpful to have a few ideas of the kind of gifts that might make sense.

WHEN "FREE" IS COSTLY

If you don't believe me when I say "free" is not always free, do an online search for the term *free checking*. I did and came up with more than 47 million references. They had all sorts of names: "No-fee checking." "Free checking." "Bonus checking." "$100 cash back." "Never pay for checks again!" Often, when you dig into the details, you find out you need to keep a large balance in the account.

The large balance represents assets not growing for you. The account typically earns little or no interest, and if the balance exceeds a reasonable cash reserve for you, it actually costs you in lost opportunity.

Investment and savings returns you can't see without a telescope are only part of the problem. Banks usually try to up sell you other products, include certificates of deposit (CDs) paying you very little. Or they'll send you to a partner representative, who, by the way, doesn't work *for* the bank, but is *in* the bank to sell you something that might be riskier than you understand, all so that you can get free checking!

WHAT SHOULD YOU DO?

If you run across one of these marketing ploys, do yourself a favor: Take the money your bank insists you keep in its account for free checking, and look for an alternative. With a little research, you'll find lots of financial institutions offering free checking if you direct deposit your paycheck.

Being proactive takes time and energy, but it will save you money. Companies know many customers won't bother to look around. Setting up new online banking arrangements or cable television services is a hassle. It's up to you to decide whether the one-time hassle is worth it.

LIFE'S BIGGEST EXPENSES

What financial consumers lose by earning near-zero interest from banks is nothing compared to the bundled charges a mortgage lender may bury you under. No money up front? You'll pay for it on the back end, along with all sorts of fees. Shop around if you're looking for a first mortgage or refinancing. It could save you thousands.

College costs are becoming a close second to home ownership expenses. How to save and pay for college are probably the toughest choices parents make. A poor plan for school is a plan not to retire when you thought. Although we may start out with the best intentions, other competing goals can get in the way. Maybe it's a bigger house, adding that deck you wanted, or buying that time share you saw on vacation. All of these ideas might enhance your enjoyment of life today, and it's hard to choose something in the future over joy today. If you don't believe me, ask any dieter.

When their kids are small, many people tell me how their children will need to have "skin in the game," how they won't pay for a four-year party. They say a state school is fine because it worked for them.

Maybe they don't save enough for the top schools. Then the kids grow older, and parents are lured by the sales pitches of many top schools. Worse yet, they buy into the myth that almost any college is affordable when you consider financial aid.

Company Stock: When Too Much of a Good Thing Becomes a Financial Landmine

Around the turn of this century, Enron was worth almost $100 per share. Its employees loved the company and its stock, until the stock fell below $1 a share and Enron went bankrupt. WorldCom and Tyco International followed suit, as their stock prices plummeted to almost nothing. All of this happened in the span of two years. Investors lost billions of dollars, and many employees of these companies lost their jobs and life savings.

Their stories are real-life tragedies. Many lost their life savings because they were so heavily invested in their company's stock. Everybody on the *Titanic* believed the ocean liner wouldn't sink because lives depended on it. Everyone who worked for or invested in Enron believed the company would always thrive, because their current and future livelihoods depended on it. No one told them otherwise. Maybe this wasn't overconfidence, but it was naivety. They learned the hard way.

Federal regulations now exist designed to prevent what happened to the employees who worked for these companies. Companies that match employees' 401(k) contributions may still make that match in company stock, but employees generally may reallocate the match elsewhere.

While it's harder to repeat the Enron travesty, you can still accumulate too much stock if you don't pay attention. Keep your company stock to a maximum of 20% of your investment assets. Don't put all your eggs into one proverbial basket. You'll be happy you did in retirement.

What they don't know is that most aid comes in the form of student and parent loans. They don't know that this *aid* really means they and their children need to borrow—and pay back—more money. Can you say, "later retirement"?

Our penchant for putting off things that help us meet long-term goals is common, but it is not helpful to long-term financial causes like paying for college or buying a home. We always think we have more time to plan, more time to save, even when we now know that time can be an ally when we use it early.

So, try this: Embrace the idea of learning about anything that can affect your financial well-being. You needn't get a PhD in finance, but you can learn the basics about the big expenses you will face in life: a home, college education, and retirement.

Quick Guide 5: Bank Account Charges and Fees: Piling on Your Costs

Shopping for a bank can be exhausting because it can hit you up for fees in so many areas. The following table shows what services typically come attached to fees and which ones usually do not. After learning about your bank's products, check off whether you need or don't need them.

Table 3. Bank fees

Bank Fees: You Pay and Then You Pay Some More				
Bank products/charges	Minimum Balance?	Need?	Don't need?	Free?
Bill pay				No
Bounced check charge				Always*
Cashier's check				Always
Checking account				Increasingly
Debit card				Rarely
Direct deposit				No
Credit card foreign transactions				Usually
Lost debit card				Sometimes
Minimum daily balance (falling below)				Yes
Overdraft protection				Usually
Paper statement				Increasingly
Returned deposit fee				Yes
Credit card rewards redemption				Sometimes
Stop payment				Always
Wire transfer				Usually

*Unless you have overdraft protection.

(Bank fees differ across the country, and some customers will pay different fees at the same bank according to how much business they do with the bank.)

Quick Guide 6: The Four Things You Should Consider Before Buying a Home

Thinking of buying a home? Consider the following:

1. **Don't buy a house unless you can stay at least five years.** I bought a house in the mid-1980s as home prices soared and my marriage faltered. Agents told me real estate always goes up, but values declined. I bought into the hype, real estate values continued to fall, and my marriage ended. So much for "real estate never goes down." Lessons learned.

2. **Pay attention to your cold feet during hot real estate markets.** My first real estate recession was nothing compared to what many people went through two decades later. Real estate values crashed—some more than 50–70 percent in places like the Northeast, Florida, and Nevada in 2005–9. Thousands had "underwater mortgages," those with balances higher than their home values. Countless bankruptcies followed as consumers couldn't pay their mortgages or sell their homes. Real estate has recovered, but the lesson remains: don't buy at the top of a hot market.

3. **It's about more than your mortgage payment.** When you buy a home, you'll likely pay fees for an application, home appraisal, surveying, credit reports, title search, title insurance, closing, settlement, recording, and attorneys. You may also pay points. After you close, you have real estate taxes and insurance that can add at least $1,000 per month for an average-priced home in major metro areas. If you didn't put 20 percent down on your home, you may also pay for private mortgage insurance, which can cost hundreds more per month. Don't forget water and sewer charges, trash pickup charges, and home maintenance.

4. **When renting makes sense.** You have large student debt you want to pay down first. You're saving to get married. You are in a career that moves you around the country. You don't want to own the home with a loved one, a family member, or a friend. When purchase prices are so much more than rents, it also might make sense to rent.

Quick Guide 7: Five of My Favorite Places to Learn about Personal Finance

If you take my advice and become willing to learn, it's important to find reputable sources that will help you understand everything from credit card fees to complex investing approaches. I have a few favorites that might interest you:

1. **Kiplinger (www.kiplinger.com).** *Kiplinger's Finance* is good, general-purpose personal finance monthly magazine and online presence.
2. **Feed the Pig (www.feedthepig.org).** An easy-to-understand website meant for beginner to intermediate financial consumers, from the American Institute of CPAs.
3. **Nerd Wallet (www.nerdwallet.com).** Among the relative new-comers, it also has plentiful information about a variety of financial topics.
4. **Credit Karma (www.creditkarma.com).** If you're looking to understand credit or for a low-interest credit card, you can find information here.
5. **Mint (www.mint.com).** By the tax and accounting software people Intuit, this is a nice general finance site.

Four

Habit 3: Establish Guideposts

Helping people through financial planning has changed a lot in twenty-five years. In the past, I would sit down with new clients and begin advising them by looking at a forensic accounting of all assets, breaking down every dollar they spent. I would ask how much they spent monthly on a hairdresser, prescription drugs, and cable television. The list went on and on. I didn't leave much out.

This process was cumbersome and frustrated most clients, but I thought it was necessary to figure out expenses to the penny to create a "book," which is a financial plan, for my clients. It wasn't long before some clients told me they gave educated guesses to what they spent and what they thought they would need in the future.

Funny thing was, though, the guessers did as well as those who counted every penny. As a result, I changed my approach and adopted guideposts to help my clients figure out their financial futures, and I recommend you do the same with your own finances.

It's easy to fail to follow a rigid budget, making it hard to forgive ourselves and to dust ourselves off and start again. Working with guideposts is a different story.

A guidepost is an estimated range of what each goal, each expense, in your life costs—or will cost in the future. They are more than suggestions but definitely less than commands. Guideposts differ from strict budgeting because they're intuitive.

You would like to retire at sixty, but would accept a range of sixty to sixty-three for this goal. You would like to keep your grocery bill to less than $150 per week, but you'll settle for $150–$170. These are basic examples of setting guideposts, which work as well to help people save for a home or an emergency fund as they do for a grocery bill.

THE PERILS OF ALL OR NOTHING

With guideposts, you move in the direction of your goal even if you can't make it all the way there. Guideposts offer a better way for two reasons:

1. **No one is perfect, and perfect planning fails perfectly the first time it's not perfect.** If you were among those people planning to retire in 2008, before the bottom dropped out of the market, you experienced a financial catastrophe that obliterated any plans. Those who had a range of ages for when they wanted to retire overcame the setback. Others put themselves on what I call a thirty-year money diet—a strict budget for less than they had anticipated having—because they had decided age sixty-two was when they would retire. They were not going to work another day, market plunges notwithstanding. Perfect planning failed people on a money diet.

   Using guideposts works on a few different levels. In the case of my clients who worked a little longer after the market collapsed, they continued to earn an income and put more money toward retirement. This extra time gave the market a chance to revive and let them recoup some of their losses. In addition, they decided not to spend money like they would have during the beginning of retirement because they were still working.

   Add it up, and you have an imperfect but perfectly doable solution. My happiest clients didn't mind working a couple of extra years because guideposts gave them a range of when they would retire. They retired happily, and with a lot more money to spend than those who refused to consider guideposts.

2. **Budgets often demand you oversave, but guideposts are realistic.** There's another reason I'm a big believer in guideposts. I believe in establishing sane financial cushions to help you accomplish common financial objectives, such as more travel in retirement. However, many financial types border on hysteria when talking about the need to plan and save ridiculous sums for long-term goals, including long-term care and retirement. Let me tell you, these people are terrifying some of my friends and clients.

Financial firms often run advertising and present information as if the world is going to end if you don't save for every possible scenario. Let's take retirement as an example. I'm not minimizing the fact that many Americans are not financially prepared for a long retirement, but going to the other extreme isn't necessary either. One company runs commercials that have toilet paper illustrating how long people can expect to live; only one rolls past the age of one hundred.

OK, I get it. Some people live that long. But, really, how many will? Do you plan for that possibility, even when you have to defy the odds to get there? And if you live that long, do you think you'll spend a lot of money then?

RETIREMENT IS NOT THE SAME FROM BEGINNING TO END

There are two problems with the toilet paper scenario. First, while Americans are living longer, only a very small percentage of Americans live past age one hundred. There were 72,197 Americans aged one hundred or more in 2014. As impressive as that number is, it is only 0.2 percent of the total population of Americans who were age sixty-five or older. In 2014, there were 46.2 million Americans age sixty-five and older. So, the odds are prohibitive that you'll live to be a hundred, despite what the toilet paper people might want you to believe.

Second, and this is more important than how long you will live, is *how* you will live. Retirement—however many years it may wind up being—is not one, constant event. Studies and real-life examples show that it comes in at least two stages.

One stage is the beginning of retirement, when you may actually spend more money than you did while working—doing all the bucket list things you never had the time to do before. This is a time, depending on health, when people are willing and able to take extra vacations, eat out more often, and generally do the things they always wanted to do but never had the time for. For my clients who have the resources, I recommend they allocate an extra $10,000–$20,000 of income for each of their first ten retirement years.

The second stage is the rest of retirement. As we age, we slow down. Maybe you do not go out to eat as often. Maybe you are hitting the early bird specials, and now you're bringing home the leftovers to eat the next night. Perhaps your vacations aren't as far, as long, or as frequent. Aging is natural. No one can stop Mother Time. On the plus side, the less we do, the less we spend.

BEND BUT NOT BREAK

Guideposts are commonsense tools that work because they help you see the big picture, because they bend but don't break. With guideposts, you estimate the things you *must have*, *don't really need*, and *don't need at all*. Then, put them in separate silos. Work from there.

This is deterministic planning. What actions should you take to reach specific goals? Let's look at common financial concerns throughout the generations and how consumers in each generation might deal with them.

MILLENNIALS (AND SOON, GENERATION Z)

You *must have* the rent. If you run short, maybe you get a second job or work overtime. Maybe neither is an option, and you cut back on expenses, such as the *don't-really-need* things like dinners out. In the extreme, you move to a place with lower rent or enlist a roommate. For every situation, there is a solution.

Know, though, that life is fluid. Events change all the time. Perhaps you pay your rent more easily, so you begin to save for a wedding. You want all the bells and whistles, but they cost a fortune—especially in major metropolitan areas. So maybe you scrimp and save some more. Perhaps you work a second job. Or maybe you realize you don't really need the wedding to end all weddings, so you downsize your expectations and the resulting expenses. You just established guideposts for a lower-cost wedding that you'll still remember a lifetime, and you do it without having a nervous breakdown. Problem solved.

Same thing with putting away a down payment for your first home. Use guideposts to estimate a percentage of income you can put in relatively safe investments. Put raises, bonuses, and windfalls into your first-home kitty, too. *Don't* look at houses above your price range. *This is crucial.* It's hard to fall in love with a house in your price range once you fall in love with more.

If you can't afford the house near work, look farther away where housing costs are less. Weigh your choices. Easy commute and less house? Or longer commute and bigger house? You have choices. Use guideposts to help you make the right choice.

Generation X and Beyond

These choices become more complex with age. Maybe you're buying a first home, saving for retirement, or putting money away for your children's college. You get older, and you might have all of these expenses, plus maybe you haven't saved enough for either retirement or college costs, and now your parents are reaching the age where they may need long-term care.

Prioritize, and then develop a strategy in which you create and contribute to virtual buckets for each financial goal.

Talk to your high school child about how much college you can really afford. Maybe you have enough to pay Junior's way through a midtier university, and the rest is up to him. How much money you will need to live comfortably in retirement is up to you. But remember that real estate taxes never go down, and health insurance premiums always cost more. Life changes. So will your goals. Save accordingly.

Then life *really* changes when a parent needs long-term care. If your parents need care, you might work fewer hours to care for them at home. Or maybe you're helping to pay for care—with limited financial resources. Either way, this will affect what you save for other goals. Adjust what you contribute to each bucket for life's unexpected emergencies.

Even when new expenses arise and you have a fixed amount of dollars to save, you have options. Your eventual answers may not be your first or second choice, but guideposts give you the flexibility to change when change occurs.

The Talk: Making a College Choice That Works for You and Your Kids

For those of you whose children have their hearts set on attending the most expensive schools, sit down with them and discuss the details. Colleges constantly tout the amount of student aid they offer, but a good portion of that aid comes in the form of loans, which you and your child will have to pay back.

Grants and work-study are the only types of aid not requiring repayment. Schools typically offer grants to lower-income families and students with exceptional academic or athletic potential. Everything else is a loan that either you or your child will have to repay. That's student aid in a nutshell.

Armed with this information, multiply your net annual costs by four—and increasingly, five—years, and then determine who can pay for what and when. Ultimately, you can always borrow for college, but you can't borrow for retirement. There are times you must be selfish, and this could be one of them.

Your child also needs to digest the numbers before committing to huge loans. Upon leaving school and hopefully beginning careers, college graduates should know they will receive an entry-level salary. Will your child have a career lucrative enough to pay off a six-figure college loan and have anything left over? Are your children willing to put off weddings, a first home, and other financial goals to pay off their loans? Or will they live in your basement? Get answers to these hard questions.

Be Brutally Honest before Your Children Incur Too Much Debt

You don't owe your children a debt-free college education, but you do owe them the truth—most college financial aid is loans. How much college debt to carry is your child's first big financial decision? Parents are uncomfortable telling children they can't have everything they want, but it's necessary, and children are coachable. Ultimately, you'll help them make loan payments and even house them well into adulthood if your boomerang kids are overburdened with debt, because our kids' problems become our problems, too. Tell them what carrying too much college debt can mean.

EXPECT THE UNEXPECTED

Because life is nothing if not a series of surprises, I recommend building as big a cushion as possible for a few life events. For instance, I believe in building a financial cushion in the event of involuntary early retirement. That extra money is the *float* to help you deal with the unexpected. Maybe you'll have to spend the entire float. Maybe you'll spend half of it and use the rest for a bucket list item.

Know that with guideposts, you have the flexibility you need when life—and your perception of what's important—changes over time.

Quick Guide 8: The High Cost of a College Education

If you don't have unlimited means—and sometimes even if you do—it is best to consider the financial costs as soon as your kids begin kindergarten, if not sooner.

FANTASY VERSUS REALITY

I saw and continue to see many parents with young children talk about making future college choices that balance the quality of the school with cost. Years later, however, these same parents have children in high school and are looking at the most expensive, most prestigious schools. Living in New England where most of the Ivy League schools and many "Little Ivy's" are located, it's hard to escape their lure. Who doesn't want their children to have the best? Damn the cost, right?

These parents will take a psychological ride many of us will face or have already faced. Even if you are a stone-cold realist, your children may **really** want to attend that prestigious, expensive school.

This, however, is reality: The College Board's Trends in College Pricing 2016 found that the average room, board, tuition, and fees for in-state, full-time students at a four-year public college or university cost $20,090 per year for in-state residents. To think that state schools used to be the frugal option! With state budgets constantly squeezed, I don't expect we'll ever see these prices decline.

The costs for the same school year at private four-year schools averaged a whopping $45,370, and sending your child to an Ivy League school now costs more than $60,000 a year. Add another $10,000 for travel and incidentals. The costs add up quickly. And increasingly, they are paid by student loans.

THE DEBT THAT KEEPS GROWING

The United States is awash in student loans. The mean balance is more than $26,000, and 15 percent of borrowers owe more than $50,000. The *Wall Street Journal* reported that the class of 2016 averaged more than

$37,000 in student loans. About two of every ten borrowers have a blemish, such as a late payment, on their records, and 17 percent are now delinquent or in default.

Of course, no one is average. Students coming from a middle-class family that didn't have the resources but sent their child to a private university could find debts over $100,000 for a bachelor's degree. To start off as a professional with this amount of debt can be a huge burden. Monthly payments can be in the hundreds of dollars. You can get an estimate from the Department of Education's repayment estimator.

HOW MANY COLLEGE APPLICATIONS ARE ENOUGH?

So where do you begin to trim costs? Start small by attacking the college application carousel. UCLA found that the percentage of students who applied to eight or more colleges more than doubled to 28.5 percent of all full-time students. Is that really necessary?

Applying for admission is not free. Application fees averaged forty-one dollars for the school year 2015–16, and some are approaching one hundred dollars. Now multiply that by eight, ten, or a dozen. Don't forget to throw in the cost of road trips to visit schools out of your area. You can see that even the cost of just exploring college costs can dent your wallet before you pay the first dollar of tuition and room and board.

Compromise on what you and your children consider a fair number of college applications. Throw out those schools that are extreme long shots. Have a first, second, and third choice, and don't forget to include a safety valve school. Liberal arts or specialized curriculum? Small or big school? Include all the variables.

IN A NUTSHELL: COLLEGE IS A JOINT FINANCIAL DECISION

Once your student chooses a school, treat college costs as purchases, not a dream, fantasy, or experience. You can't put yourself in bankruptcy over this. Be honest about what you can afford to help with, and work with your student to ensure a realistic look at future financial prospects—with and without a ton of college debt. For more information, check out the Department of Education's <u>College Preparation Checklist</u>.

Quick Guide 9: How to Pay for College and Not Destroy Your Retirement

You can always borrow for college, but you can't borrow for retirement. That's not to say you should bury yourself in parent loans, either. Here are some ways to pay for your child's college education.

COLLEGE SAVINGS PLANS

The best way to meet college costs is to save early and regularly, but at least save something. Here are a few ways to accomplish this and get tax advantages in the process:

1. **529 plan.** Named after a section of the Internal Revenue tax code, 529 plans are actually two plans. The first, less common option is a prepaid plan, in which you pay future costs typically at a discount of what college will cost in the future. This is less common because your future student usually must attend the schools sponsoring the plan or one of the schools eligible in specific state plans.

    The second 529 plan is a savings program you can use for future student education costs for any person at any eligible school. You get a choice of investments, typically mutual funds, into which you put your contributions. Some states allow state tax deductions on contributions, potential investment earnings are tax deferred, and benefits used to pay eligible expenses are tax-free.

    The plan's impact on potential financial aid is generally low, as long as a student is not owner of the plan. Account owners control the money in a 529 plan and may transfer it for use by other college students. Ineligible withdrawals are subject to a 10 percent tax penalty.

2. **Education savings account (ESA).** If you qualify by income, you can put up to $2,000 into an ESA. Earnings grow tax-deferred,

and eligible withdrawals are tax-free. When owned by a parent, an ESA does not have an adverse effect on the estimated family contribution to college, but it will negatively affect aid if the student owns it. One unique feature is that you can use the savings to pay for elementary and secondary schools, too. Penalties apply for ineligible withdrawals.

OTHER WAYS TO SAVE

Some parents put college money into a Uniform Gifts to Minors Act (UGMA) or Uniform Transfers to Minors Act (UTMA) account. The challenges, however, are numerous. Once your child reaches age eighteen (or twenty-one in some states), they have control over the funds. The problem is when you save it, your child is young and you are brimming with the possibilities. Sometimes, though, later on, not so much! By the time you figure it out, the funds might be gone.

You might also save money in an investment account in your own name. There aren't any tax incentives to saving it here, but you do have the right to use this money however you choose.

CUT EXPENSES EARLY

Another way to manage college is to work to reduce costs. Have your child take advanced placement courses in high school, which some colleges accept as college credit. Have him or her the CLEP test, which grants credit for life experiences. Your child could go to a less expensive state school or community college for a fraction of what the most expensive private universities cost. You can usually transfer credits for core subjects needed at any four-year school. Have your child commute during freshman and sophomore years, forgoing the experience and $6,000–$10,000 annually in room and board costs.

If you must borrow funds as a parent for your child's college, try to pay the least amount of interest.

Refinancing a first mortgage or taking a second mortgage to pay may stretch out the length of your mortgage; however, at least the interest will likely be deductible, and the rates are typically 4–6 percent cheaper than a Parent PLUS loan.

PAUSE ON YOUR RETIREMENT SAVINGS

By the time your child goes to college, you are likely within a few years of your retirement. It can be painful to reduce or stop savings for retirement in order to manage a college payment plan, but if you are well funded for retirement, this could be a way to reduce or avoid interest payments.

HAVE YOUR CHILD SAVE AND WORK

Any assets or income your child makes will be considered 100 percent available for his or her education, but if we go back to remembering that most students end up with loans anyway, we might be willing to give up the dream of not paying and get onto figuring out how to pay. Work in the summer and save for books as well as discretionary expenses once in school? This is a great idea, and one most parents should consider.

PAY FOR COLLEGE OUT OF POCKET

If you're fortunate enough to be at or near the peak of your career, and your income is predictably rising, you may be able to pay for at least some college costs out of pocket. The downside? You probably won't qualify for much financial aid.

STUDENT AID

You can do everything right and still need to tap some student aid. The trick is to try to make any loans you or your child take manageable. If you expect any aid, you first need to complete the Free Application for Federal Student Aid (FAFSA). Go to fafsa.ed.gov for answers to some of your questions.

Colleges typically offer three types of aid: grants, loans, and work study. You must pay back loans. There are federal and private college loans; choose the former whenever possible, as they will likely offer you the best interest rates and more favorable payment options, including longer terms.

In addition to the federal government, which is the largest student loan lender, most states offer some aid in the form of grants and loans. Some states, for example, offer money to keep top-performing high school students in state. Colleges and universities also offer grants for certain majors, academic excellence, and sports. Be aware, however, that grants are often for one year and may not be renewable.

The federal government offers a variety of mostly needs-based grants, such as the Pell Grant and grants for students who are veterans or who will become teachers in certain areas. Students may also apply for grants as members of military families, for community service, and even for their heritage.

Federal loan service and lending company Sallie Mae has a searchable database with millions of scholarships. Also, check out thousands of financial aid opportunities, including grants and fellowships, through the Department of Education and private sites including www.fastweb.com and www.finaid.org. Beware of scam artists, and carefully vet any person or organization charging a fee to help you find aid, especially when you can probably do this on your own.

Five

Habit 4: Take Charge

You're on an airline flight, and before the plane takes off, the attendant instructs you to put the oxygen mask on yourself before helping others in an emergency. For women, this is especially poignant because our first instinct is always to help others—our children, our family, and our friends. Helping ourselves first is not a natural act.

What is undeniable, though, is that you can't help others to the best of your ability unless you help yourself first. This is especially true in your financial life. Taking charge of your finances is a choice—*your* choice.

Should you choose to take charge of your personal finances, career prospects, and retirement planning, there are steps you can take to help the process along. Let's look at them one step at a time.

YOUR PERSONAL FINANCES

The first step in establishing and maintaining a strong personal financial picture is to create an atmosphere of order. You begin to take charge when you *organize*.

- **Open your mail.** I know this sounds crazy, but you would be amazed at how many clients I have who don't open their mail. A couple of women come to my office a few times a year with bags of unopened financial mail containing bank statements, retirement plan information, investment accounts, credit cards, and more. Sometimes I find checks and, one time, a rebate check for an insurance payment made twice. You *must* open your mail.

- **As important, you actually have to read the mail you open.** You'll find countless reasons in this chapter alone why this is so important. I know we all set mail aside intending to read it later, but then life gets in the way, and we forget. Make it a habit to read your mail as soon as you open it. You never know when you might find time-sensitive information.

- **Take care of your mail.** Give it a proper burial—the only proper burial—by shredding it when no longer needed. While cyber theft makes all the headlines, there are still more than a few cases of old-fashioned stolen identity from thieves going through the trash.

- **For the mail you do keep, put all paper copies of your bills, notices, and other important items in one place.** A spreadsheet, personal accounting software program, or even a filing cabinet will work for those of you who are still old school.

- **If you use personal finance software, safeguard your information against viruses and malware.** Consider backing up your financial information and other important data on a zip drive.

- **Use password managers to back up your financial information safely.** Search respected publications like *PC Magazine* for "best password managers" for some top-rated choices. Comprehensive security software like Norton that generate (and remember) difficult-to-hack passwords will also help.

- **Don't bury your money in the backyard.** Literally and figuratively. People occasionally tell me they have money hidden somewhere in the house. I ask these people if they have fire insurance. This question never fails to shock them into thinking about a better solution.

- **Keep a checklist of all your bills and their payment due dates.** This is critical because electronic statements are difficult for some people to track. I've seen people whose life insurance policies lapsed because they inadvertently failed to make a payment.

- **Make sure a loved one or financial professional knows where to find all your important financial information.** You might, for instance, keep a note with your attorney or have a folder in a file cabinet that lists where loved ones can find anything having to do with your finances.
- **Become a *Doubting Thomas*.** When it comes to money matters, showing a healthy skepticism makes perfect sense. When you are a Doubting Thomas, you give yourself the ability to nip potential financial problems in the bud. A Doubting Thomas doesn't throw away money, and she regularly identifies how she can save more. A Doubting Thomas chooses to take charge.

A DOUBTING THOMAS IS A SMART CONSUMER

Skepticism is healthy and should be a part of every money decision you make. At the least, you can short-circuit small problems before they become big when you're a Doubting Thomas. In the extreme, you can save hundreds, if not thousands, of dollars by identifying potential problem areas.

Here's a seemingly innocuous area that can cost you money without you even knowing about it: Every year, credit card providers mail us updated terms of agreements. If you don't read these little packages of legalese, you have a ton of company, but you should at least scan them. You might learn that your interest rate is increasing. Even a 1 percent increase can cost you hundreds of dollars over time.

Or you could learn that a forgotten deadline can cost you even more. In 2016, for example, credit cards could charge a late fee of up to twenty-seven dollars for a first offense and thirty-eight dollars for a repeat offense. Congress capped these fees in the Credit CARD Act of 2009, but they can rise in line with inflation.

Late fees, though, are only the half of it. Although some major credit card issuers are doing away with the practice, others continue to hike a card's interest rate by 10 percent or more for late payments or for exceeding credit limits.

These are some of the reasons to become a Doubting Thomas. Yes, this means reading admittedly brain-freezing terms of agreements when they come in the mail each year. These aren't, however, the only reasons.

If you have taken advantage of a retailer's no-interest-for-x-amount-of-months sales enticers, you're not alone. There is nothing inherently wrong with these deals, but be aware of their implications. As good as a no-interest offer sounds, some of them end with a financial time bomb. You might make minimum payments with no interest charged for maybe twelve months, and then you begin paying interest—all of it!

A Doubting Thomas will figure this out and make sure to pay the balance in full during the no-interest window instead of making minimum payments. A Doubting Thomas who takes charge of her finances might even go a step further, negotiating with the retailer for a lower price for cash, leaving her money for other necessities.

Now, let's take this healthy skepticism in a different direction. Let's say you make an honest mistake and forget to put a credit card payment in the mail. The card issuer's terms of agreement say you must make that late payment with penalty, but you shouldn't accept this as fact. Call the customer service number and ask the representative to revoke the penalty. More times than not, card carriers will waive the late charge for customers with no previous late payments.

And while you're on the phone, take charge and ask the card issuer for its best interest rate. Negotiate! These rates, as most costs in life, are negotiable.

GO ALONG TO GET ALONG

Maybe it's the nurturer in us, but women don't seem to have the enthusiasm to negotiate as much as men do. While we would rather go along and get along, we don't live in this type of world. You'll find times when you need your negotiation skills in the mundane, everyday existence of your life. There are times when it is hurtful financially to get along, go along.

So why not try this? Don't shy away from confrontation—not when it concerns your finances. You don't have to rant and rave because you want someone to hear you. In my family, that's who we are. Sometimes you vent, just asking to be heard.

My rants get raves. But I know that when it's time to get what you deserve financially, it should involve a calm, reasoned tone of voice, a conviction that you deserve what you are asking for, and a request that is reasonable. I encourage you to negotiate, even if it's with yourself when you're mulling over financial decisions in your head.

You have the tools to help you negotiate like a master because you now have these skills:

- **You understand the unique financial circumstances of being a woman** and understand you should pay extra attention to ensure a secure future.
- **You aren't afraid to fail.** You negotiate with your credit card issuer and you calmly take your business elsewhere when you can't get a lower rate or waived fees. If you try and fail, so what? You honed your negotiation skills, which can save you thousands down the road.
- **You know a little about money,** and you apply these lessons to every financial situation. Perhaps you are mulling over buying the $200 sweater you fell in love with at the mall. However, you demonstrate your new financial awareness and become a Doubting Thomas, even if you're only negotiating with yourself. You say to the new, financially aware you, "Maybe the one-hundred-dollar sweater works just as well and looks almost as good."
- **Recognize when free isn't free.** You get twelve months' interest-free financing to buy furniture you didn't intend to buy. That's not free. Or you buy two pairs of shoes—one of which is wildly expensive—because you got one free. That's not free either,

because you didn't need two pairs of shoes for one marked-up price. Retailers offer carrots like these all the time. You have a choice. Eat the carrot the retailer dangles and buy something you really didn't need, or learn to shop like a ninja—have a plan, and execute it quickly and wisely. Find what you need, grab it, and get out!

Once you recognize these financial traps and learn how to avoid them, and you understand the fundamentals that bring sanity to your personal finances, why not take a new look at your career?

TAKING CHARGE IN THE WORKPLACE

When it comes to what you want in your career, negotiate! There's that word again. Embrace the discomfort or, better yet, learn to accept a little discomfort. Negotiate for a better salary. In the best case, you're worth it and will receive a higher salary. In the worst case, you make less than a man performing the exact same job. Even without the traditional burden of providing care for loved ones, women continue to battle for equal footing—financial and otherwise—with men in the workplace.

It doesn't have to be this way.

Negotiation doesn't include threatening to leave if your employer refuses to meet your demands, but you should keep looking for a new job as a silent option if your demands are not met satisfactorily. Holding a proverbial gun to an employer's head may get you temporary satisfaction. It isn't, however, a great way to further your career in the same organization, even if you get the raise you deserve.

If you aren't happy and you don't get what you merit from your current employer, find a new one. Just don't broadcast your job search. Remember that it's easier to get a job if you have a job.

Understand that finding an employer who values you will involve future negotiations. If you find a job you like and don't get the offer you want, why not say "no" and move on to your next opportunity? There are other fish in the pond, other companies that will value what you offer.

You *will* eventually find an employer who recognizes your value in monetary terms, not just in words. Just don't be afraid to take charge, to ask for what you're worth. Take the same well-reasoned, methodical approach to your career that you do in other financial areas of your life. After all, your career is likely the centerpiece of your financial picture.

OLDER JOB CHANGERS

A quick note: advancing age increases the difficulties of finding a job. During the 2008 recession, I had many conversations with older workers worried that their jobs would be eliminated. Many of them were right. We talked about immediately beginning a job if they were worried about the long-term viability their current job, but most people failed to do this—and the same is true now. Why? Older workers can tell you how they are discriminated against in the marketplace due to age, and they fear that they will end up answering to some know-nothing young boss. I often see older workers who go down with the *Titanic* because inertia and fear have frozen them. But if you know your job is ending, why wait to the bitter end?

If you believe your current position or, for that matter, your company is headed toward oblivion, don't go down with the ship. Work with a specialist to refresh your resume and take charge of your job search immediately. Consult a career counselor. You may find opportunities you never knew existed.

EMBRACE DISCOMFORT, EMBRACE CHANGE

Throughout this chapter, I have emphasized the power of taking charge. This comes with discomfort if you aren't used to even minor confrontation, but you should understand that discomfort is relative.

Real discomfort is not having enough money to retire when you want to because of loans you made to friends or loved ones who didn't repay them.

Discomfort is borrowing heavily from your 401(k) plan or not contributing at all while you scrounge for every dollar to help children through the very best and most expensive schools.

Women Aren't Equal to Men in the Workplace (Psst...They're Better)

There are still Neanderthals masquerading as business owners and bosses, people who think women can't do the same job as men. Two women in Iceland not only shattered this perception, they did better. They proved that feminine values bring awareness and an important perspective to business.

In 2007, Halla Tómasdóttir and Kristín Pétursdóttir founded Audur Capital in Iceland. A year later, when the Great Recession struck, they were the last bankers standing in this tiny country. These women survived in a male-dominated profession where others did not.

In a TED Talk titled *A Feminine Response to Iceland's Financial Crash*, Tómasdóttir talked about how her company's success was due, in part, to "feminine values." She believes the world would benefit from more gender balance, especially in business.

That balance is encompassed in five core feminine values. The first, risk awareness, means not investing in things you don't understand. It doesn't mean not taking risks; it means understanding risks. The other core feminine values are profit with principles, emotional capital, straight talking, and independence.

These core values worked for Audur Capital, which was the only private banker in Iceland to survive the financial crisis. Audur merged with another company, Virding, in 2014. Today, Pétursdóttir is chief executive officer of Virding. Tómasdóttir ran for the Icelandic presidency, finishing second, and runs a handful of companies.

Theirs is one story, albeit a high-profile one, that proves a woman doesn't—and, in fact, shouldn't—act like a man to be financially successful.

Their story is one of many that proves women don't have to take a back seat to anyone.

Discomfort is if you never saved anything, and suddenly you're reaching retirement age and want to continue working but can't physically do so.

Like I said, discomfort is relative. But discomfort now can lead to future comfort, such as when you have the temporary discomfort of *not buying* things you really don't need, so you can add 1 percent to your retirement account.

In these and every other area of our lives, a little discomfort can provide comfort when we need it later. I'm not asking you to take a vow of poverty, but you can embrace discomfort within reason. You can embrace minor and temporary discomfort to make the decisions that are right for you and your future.

Embrace taking charge of your finances. Then, think about how empowered you will feel when you take charge by negotiating for what is right. Empowerment can become a little addictive, and you'll be the one telling your friends to call the bank and negotiate a rate change because it worked for you and wasn't that difficult. This is taking charge.

It's your choice.

Block the Rabbit Hole Entrance before Lending Money to Family and Friends

In the film *Alice through the Looking Glass*, Alice experiences adventures that are confusing and unexpected. When you enter the rabbit hole that is lending money to family and friends, you can have an experience that feels just as overwhelming as Alice's—or worse. Lending money is often the quickest way to turn loved ones into former friends and estranged family.

I see it happen all the time. Women are seen as the soft touch, so people find it easier to ask us for money. And we give. I've seen more than one person nearing retirement withdraw money from an IRA and lend it to a cousin, only to never see it again.

What did they receive in return? A more financially difficult retirement and permanently damaged relationships. Just as the airline attendants imply with their oxygen-mask speech, you can't help others unless you help yourself first. You aren't helping yourself by depleting your retirement money in this way.

I understand that not loaning to family and friends in need may be uncomfortable at first, but the discomfort you feel when you say no is OK. It's temporary, and certainly better than the discomfort you could feel if you run out of money in retirement.

If you are going to lend money to family and friends, do so with the mind-set that you may never see this money again. When I'm asked for money, I say, "I will lend you this money, but I don't want to be the family bank. It would be great if you pay me back, but if you do not, I will never speak about it again. I don't want to chase you for the money. But if you do not pay me back, I will never lend you money again, so please don't ask."

Lend money because you can afford it. If you don't get the money back, you're prepared, and you won't damage relationships.

Quick Guide 10: Take Charge by Taking Full Advantage of Your Employee Benefits

Most of us would like to invest the maximum allowed in as many retirement accounts as possible and carry all the insurance we need to protect against just about any risk, but we often can't afford it all. That's where employee benefits can help, a one-stop-shopping type of experience. This cost-effective way to buy insurance and save for retirement is one reason to pay close attention during open enrollment if you are employed by a company that offers these benefits—or if you are the employer who offers benefits to employees.

Open enrollment is a time when you can buy, switch, or drop your benefits. Employer-provided group insurance typically costs less than individual insurance in the workplace. You make pretax contributions, meaning Uncle Sam helps you pay for some of these benefits.

HEALTH INSURANCE: YOUR INDISPENSABLE BENEFIT

Health insurance is fast becoming one of our most expensive necessities, and costs continue to increase. Consider the following tips to make the best decision for you and your loved ones:

1. **Pick a policy from a network that includes your health providers.** We value our personal health providers, and understandably so. Buying a less expensive policy may save you premium dollars, but it will cost much more in out-of-pocket expenses if your providers are not in the network.

2. **Know your out-of-pocket costs**. Premium payments are only part of your costs. In 2016, the average deductible for a high-deductible health plan (HDHP) was more than $2,000, according to the Kaiser Family Foundation. After deductibles, you may also have coinsurance equaling 20 percent of the next few thousand dollars. Some also have copayments, a set dollar amount you pay when you buy prescription drugs or see a doctor.

HDHPs don't have to cap out-of-pocket costs until they reach $6,550 for individuals and $13,100 for families in a given year, so it's important to know all of your costs.

3. **Take advantage of a health savings account (HSA).** Only owners of HDHPs qualify for an HSA, which allows contributions up to $3,350 for individual coverage and $6,750 for family coverage annually. This can help you pay for out-of-pocket and other qualified health expenses. An HSA is triple tax-free. Contributions are deducted pretax, potential investment gains are tax-free, and qualified payments are tax-free. You can also roll over leftover money from year to year.

RETIREMENT PLAN BENEFIT: YOUR FINANCIAL FUTURE

While you may value health insurance most, the availability of a 401(k) plan or other qualified retirement plan is crucial to Americans' ability to achieve a financially secure retirement.

In a qualified plan, you make tax-deferred contributions, which employers almost always automatically deduct from your paycheck. You choose among the investment options your employer offers, and potential gains are tax deferred. You pay ordinary income taxes on withdrawals, typically after age fifty-nine and a half.

Most withdrawals made before age fifty-nine and a half are subject to a 10 percent penalty tax, but some withdrawals (up to certain limits), including permanent disability or the down payment on a first home, are penalty-free. I believe that no investment can serve two masters, so it's best to have a strategy for each financial goal or emergency. That said, there are times when it's nice to have the flexibility.

One final note about company-provided 401(k) plans, SIMPLE plans, 403(b) plans, and 457 plans. If you have one of the latter three plans, you know they operate like a 401(k) plan with a few differences. If one of the latter three is not available from your employer, don't worry if you don't understand them. You can only access them through the workplace.

Your employer can (or must, in the case of some SIMPLE plans) match part of your contributions to any qualified plan. That's why one of the strongest pieces of advice I can give you is to contribute at least as much to your plan as your employer will match and never leave free money on the table.

LIFE INSURANCE

The other common benefit most organizations offer their employees is term life insurance, which pays a predetermined benefit only upon the death of the insured person. Larger companies typically offer and pay for base coverage, usually from $5,000 to $25,000, and may allow employees to purchase more.

Employers are increasingly offering group whole life insurance as an employee benefit, typically with a nominal amount of coverage that doesn't require an application, regardless of your current or past health. However, additional coverage requires underwriting to determine your eligibility and cost. The insurer could investigate your health history via an application and potentially a physical exam.

DISABILITY INCOME INSURANCE

Employers may also offer disability income (DI) insurance. This coverage protects most people's greatest asset—their ability to earn a living. Studies show that employees are much more likely to experience a long-term disability than to die during their working years.

DI insurance typically pays 60–70 percent of gross income, minus state or federal disability benefits paid. Its cost through the workplace is typically less expensive than if you buy it on your own.

LONG-TERM CARE INSURANCE

Larger organizations are also offering long-term care insurance to their employees. This insurance doesn't cover medical costs or replace your income, but it will pay for the cost of long-term care. Some care, such as services provided by a home health aide, can be relatively inexpensive. At the other extreme, care in a nursing home can cost $10,000 or more per month, depending on where you live.

The best time to buy this coverage is between ages fifty and sixty, because premiums increase dramatically after that. If you don't have other assets to pay for this type of care, long-term care insurance can help you meet some of the costs.

AND THERE'S MORE

Most smaller employers offer a few of these basic benefits, but larger organizations are offering all sorts of extra benefits, including pet insurance, car-buying services, and adoption assistance.

Your task during open enrollment? Decide what you really need, the cost for each, and how much take-home income you'll be left with if you buy these benefits. Understand that these benefits provide a good foundation, but they may not provide all the protection and savings opportunities you need. Also know that just because your employer offers a benefit doesn't mean you must buy it. Spend your benefit dollars wisely on what you need.

Quick Guide 11: Take Charge by Planning for Your Retirement

When I write a headline like this, I can only imagine the collective eye roll younger people give to this notion of planning for something that seems a million miles away. I'm not a hysterical doomsayer telling you the end of the world is near if you don't begin to plan for retirement right now. I am, however, here to tell you that tomorrow comes around much faster than you could ever imagine.

Planning is essential when you look at the enormity of this task. You need to sort out more current financial challenges than you can count. You need to balance other long-term financial goals like paying for Junior's college or caring for parents. Planning will show how much you can save for retirement and still meet all your other current and future financial challenges. With planning, you can identify your *ultimate bargain*.

A SERIES OF BARGAINS

Your ultimate bargain is a series of smaller bargains—sort of a negotiation with yourself. One part of you—especially if you are a woman—might think you will have to work forever because you will never save enough to retire. So why bother saving for retirement at all?

Dying on the job needn't be anyone's finish. Do you know what that leaves you? A self-fulfilling prophecy. We can always *do something*. I encourage you to *do something*.

So why not start here? You *will* have Social Security, despite what the doomsayers say. It's not a lot, but it can serve as a building block. Where will you get the rest of your retirement income? Contribute to an employer-provided retirement plan. Find more money by passing on the occasional designer cup of coffee. Eat out one less time per month. There are many ways to find a few extra dollars. Consider contributing at least the amount your employer will match. Again, don't pass up the free money.

Next, ask yourself some important questions whose answers can save you money. Does Junior really have to go to the most expensive college on your dime? Can you do without the one-month European vacation when a ten-day cruise to four European countries at one-quarter of the price is more than enough? Make life's little bargains. It's not an all-or-nothing proposition.

Remember the power of time and compounding. Use them to your advantage.

If you are closer to retirement, continue to add as much to your retirement kitty as possible without living like a monk. You can live your life today and still save for tomorrow and pay down your debt. Paying off high-interest debt can give you more financial freedom than most investments can.

During all this time—from when you are young to when retirement nears—think about what you really want during retirement. If you want a travel-filled lifestyle, know you will need to save for it. If you want a bigger financial cushion, maybe you pick up a temporary job during retirement.

Life's little bargains.

Baby boomers are increasingly transitioning into retirement, not diving into it headfirst. We are living longer. If healthy, why not continue working—at least some of the time? Why buy a new car every three years when our current vehicle will treat us well for six?

THE BUCKET APPROACH

Decide what's really important in your life. I counsel my clients throughout their working lives and in retirement to break their retirement expenses into *needs* and *wants*. In one bucket, put the money you need to live—money for food, lodging, healthcare, and more.

In the other bucket, you save for wants. This includes typical bucket list items like a vacation with kids and grandkids to Disney World or maybe a cruise around the world. If you don't have enough money in one year to pull off one of your wants, maybe you plan a staycation one year and a dream getaway the next so you don't break the bank.

Like I said, life—like planning—is a series of little bargains. How you accumulate income for retirement may be your ultimate bargain. Just know that, like the Rolling Stones sing, "You can't always get what you want, but if you try sometimes, you get what you need."

Six

Habit 5: Embrace Change

Throughout this book, I address the expected financial challenges many hardworking women face. We also have those challenges that test every fiber of our being and affect every area of our lives, not just the financial end. I had one of those tests.

Sometimes, life comes at you fast and unexpectedly. In the summer of 2008, my business was growing quickly, and I was in the best shape of my life at forty-five years old. I felt almost invincible as I began the Timberman Triathlon, a 70.3-mile Ironman race.

I remember coming out of the swimming portion of the race feeling a little dizzy. I had injured an artery in my neck during the swim, but I didn't know that, so I took off my wetsuit and hopped on my bike to start some righteous hill climbing.

My heart rate climbed with the hills when, fifteen miles into the fifty-six-mile ride, I felt the worst-ever wave of pain hit my head. I thought I had a migraine or heat stroke. (Yes, I would run through a heat stroke back then; I ran with a stress fracture for a year.) My bike wobbled a little, but I straightened it and kept riding. I am a stubborn and goal-oriented woman. Quitting is not in my DNA.

I passed up water stops to pick off some racers and completed the fifty-six miles. After GU (race food, pronounced "goo") and three Advil, I changed shoes and started the 13.1-mile run. By then, the temperature was soaring. About three miles in, I considered quitting. Then I looked around with my still-fuzzy vision, and I thought, "Suck it up, KT. Everyone looks terrible."

So, I just kept running...until my body realized I was out of my mind. I collapsed.

UNEXPECTED CHANGE

For the next three days, I lay in the cardiac intensive care unit of a small, local hospital in the lakes region of New Hampshire, projectile vomiting and passing out over and over again. Doctors thought I had a heart attack. Twice more while in the ICU, I suffered that almost unbearable wave of pain throughout my head. Only then did a night nurse figure out that I may have a neurological problem. She referred me to a neurologist, who gave me a different diagnosis.

Some thirteen miles into the biking portion of the triathlon, when I felt that first wave of indescribable pain, I suffered a stroke! In the hospital, I suffered two more.

After hearing the news, I lay in the hospital bed and knew things needed to change—and change fast.

Volunteers at the water stops in the race might have seen the signs, but I didn't stop, so they couldn't make me quit. Even before the race, there were actions I could have taken to potentially prevent the strokes. I could have reduced some of the stress in my life when it all started to seem like too much that year, but I didn't.

Immediately following the strokes, I was hospitalized for five days and then did speech, occupational, and physical therapy for four months. During those months following my strokes, I worked fifteen to twenty-five hours a week, slept ten to twelve hours a day, went to rehab, and cried a lot. A year and a half later, I felt like myself again, but I made changes to my business during that time.

The financial system collapsed three weeks after my strokes. I thought about leaving the industry but decided instead to change the way I ran the business. I hired someone to help me run my business, sold one hundred clients to another advisor, and fired my biggest client, who made unreasonable time demands that I gladly gave before but was no longer willing to give.

I embraced the change that was thrust upon me, hiring more staff and bringing in another advisor to help me manage the client relationships. My staff and business have grown substantially since then. Today, I work less than forty hours a week instead of fifty-five-plus. It was a hard choice to make, but a smart one. I do only the jobs that I am uniquely qualified for, and I trust the rest to my extremely competent team. Embracing change was positive for my business.

Embracing change also mattered personally. I worked hard to get well, and I've since competed in three 140.6-mile Ironman races. The difference between now and then is I listen more to my body and work to stay safe. I made the best of change, and so can you.

TAXES CHANGE

We can prepare for expected changes, such as retirement, but we have to deal with unexpected changes on the fly, including a change in health or taxes. As I write this chapter, the top federal income tax rate stands at 39.6 percent. However, a new president is promising to lower taxes. We'll see what happens.

Tax changes are nothing new. Three and a half decades ago, the highest federal tax bracket was 70 percent. I expect the top rate will certainly not increase by the time you read this, and it will lower if the majority party gets its way.

Top brackets are only the tip of the tax iceberg. In 2016, there were seven federal tax brackets, with the lowest standing at 10 percent. Young adults, because they're lower earners, likely pay taxes at lower rates and generally have few of the myriad deductions that can reduce taxes. Older Americans, often parents and homeowners, typically earn more. As high earners, they can take advantage of multiple tax deductions for dependent children, real estate taxes, and mortgage interest to lower their taxable rate.

Taxpayers ages fifty-five to sixty-five are usually among the highest earners and hardest hit by taxes. They often are at the peak of their earning power but often have fewer tax deductions than they had perhaps a decade earlier. Tax management is important to most people, but it is vital for this group.

Retirement savings accounts are among the most popular ways Americans manage taxes now and in the future. Contributions to most retirement plans lower current taxes because they lower the amount of income subject to taxes. As I've said before, if your employer has a 401(k) plan, take advantage of the pretax funding options, as well as potential company matches.

If, however, you don't have a 401(k) or you want another way to put money away for retirement, consider a traditional IRA. If you qualify by income, you may contribute to a traditional IRA on a pretax basis. Know, however, that once you begin taking distributions from a traditional IRA in the future, you will pay tax at whatever the tax rate is at the time on every dime you withdraw. IRA distributions also have early withdrawal rules. Although there are some exceptions, most withdrawals from a traditional IRA incur a tax penalty if taken before age fifty-nine and a half.

THE UPSIDE-DOWN IRA

There is an upside-down type of IRA, better known as the Roth IRA. This IRA works for anyone who qualifies by income, and it is particularly useful if you don't qualify for the tax deduction on traditional IRA contributions. Although you make contributions with after-tax money, everything else is tax-free—including withdrawals—if you follow a few rules.

Many people expect their tax rate to be significantly lower in retirement than in their working years, which is not always true. The Roth IRA is a great way to access income in retirement that is truly tax-free.

THE POWER OF THE ROTH CONVERSION

A good time to convert to the tax-free option is when you find yourself in a year when you have low income due to time out of the workforce. This could provide significant tax-free growth for retirement, and converting in a lower tax bracket than you saved it in gives you an immediate reduction of total taxes over your lifetime. If you're working at 30 percent and convert at 15 percent, you cut your taxes on that amount in half.

As I detailed earlier, my health challenge coincided with the greatest economic downturn in this country since the Great Depression. With unemployment rising, several of my clients lost their jobs and found themselves in a lower income bracket.

While this wasn't the change they sought, they embraced change in a positive way. Because they were in significantly lower tax brackets than when they contributed to traditional IRAs (remember, withdrawals are taxable), I worked with them to convert their accounts to Roth IRAs. During a tough financial time, the conversion provided an instant win for clients.

Interest rates also declined quickly during that time. Many of my clients and I took advantage of the rate change to refinance mortgages at lower rates, often cutting years off the duration of the loans.

TAX-FRIENDLY HEALTH SAVINGS

Before we move on to a few thoughts about investing, consider one more tax-friendly investment account that is especially useful if you expect to occupy a higher tax bracket in retirement: a health savings account (HSA). Again, I love the future tax-free aspect of this account. HSA withdrawals for qualified health expenses are tax-free. You need to pair an HSA with a high-deductible health plan, but the benefits for doing so are numerous.

When Nondeductible IRAs Are Not Your Best Choice

I'm not a big fan of contributing to a traditional IRA when you don't qualify for tax-deductible contributions. Instead, I often recommend my clients buy investments outside a traditional IRA if they don't qualify for a Roth IRA or if they already contribute the maximum to one. A look at the after-tax treatment of withdrawals from each will tell you why.

Most of my clients pay a higher rate for federal income taxes than capital gains, both before and during retirement. The top 2016 federal income tax rate was 39.6%, but most people in this income tax bracket paid 15%–20% in capital gains tax, which the Internal Revenue Service levies on investments owned for at least a year and a day.

Why risk paying a higher income tax in retirement on stocks inside a traditional IRA when you can buy the same stocks outside the retirement account and pay capital gains tax instead? Most people should strive to pay the least amount of taxes over a lifetime, not a particular year.

The bottom line is this: If all your money is tax deferred, you won't know how much you'll be taxed when you take future distributions. Why take chances? Look at your lifetime tax picture, not just a slice of your life, when choosing how to invest for retirement.

THE "TAKE"

While managing federal income taxes is important, Uncle Sam isn't the only one collecting taxes. Many states, counties, and cities levy income and sales taxes. Knowing this, investors need to not fight the "take," which is the net return earned on any investment after factoring in taxes, expenses, and sales charges. Let me give you an example.

Let's say I have an opportunity to buy two different bonds in the amount of $10,000 each. The corporate bond pays 3.5 percent, while the municipal bond pays 3 percent. The corporate bond will generate $350 annually in earnings while the municipal bond will generate $300 annually. At first blush, the corporate bond seems to be the better choice as it will earn you more money annually. But don't stop there. Take a closer look.

Let's say your state and federal income tax totals 20 percent on the corporate bond, but 0 percent on the municipal bond. Suddenly, it is better to earn less with the municipal bond because it allows you to keep the whole of your $300 in annual earnings, whereas the corporate bond only allows you to keep $280 after taxes. Good thing you stopped to examine all of the variables.

The higher your tax bracket, the more important it is to take a closer look at how taxes impact your investments. Often, investors ignore the impact of the take and miss potential income they could keep.

INVESTING FOR LONGER LIVES—WITHIN REASON

Another strategy that might sound familiar to you is "buy and hold." As an investor, however, understand that when you invest for the long term, "buy and hold" doesn't mean "buy and forget." In other words, don't ignore your investments and follow the strategy you create to determine the right investment mix.

I like at least half of most retirees' portfolios to be in stocks, with the rest in fixed income investments. Others might suggest you match your fixed income assets to your age. The latter approach, in my opinion, does not provide enough growth to accommodate longer, more active lives.

Whatever percentage you choose, you'll want a smoother ride for your investments in retirement. You may continue to buy stocks on the dip and sell high flyers because you like the view more than their prices, like investors of all ages should. However, you might take extra steps to ensure the safety of your principal. Maybe you will rebalance your portfolio two to four times a year, instead of once annually, to strictly maintain your target allocation. I also have clients who don't care about hot or bad markets and stand pat no matter what. That's why they call us individuals.

A DELICATE BALANCING ACT

Managing both safety and the need for growth is a delicate balancing act, but it doesn't mean eliminating stocks from your strategy, even in retirement. Your asset allocation should still include stocks, maybe real estate, and other growth investments. A moderately aggressive investor might have an allocation of 65 percent in stocks and 35 percent in fixed income investments as retirement begins.

Now, you might think this investment mix is dangerous because during retirement you will live off what you saved throughout your life. But consider that most retirees live longer and have a more active retirement than retirees of the past. Therefore, holding a healthy percentage of stocks in retirement can help ensure you are still earning needed money to see you through retirement. Again, it's a fine line between risky and appropriate. You can limit your risk with a comprehensive investing strategy.

Whether you're thirty-five or seventy years old, I believe investments perform best over time when you establish an investment strategy and avoid unnecessary expenses and fees. Whether you create a strategy yourself or with the help of an advisor, stick to the framework. There will be times when circumstances dictate that you embrace change and switch up your investments, but only rare times when you will need to change your strategy completely.

The latter will happen because—as we've already established—change will happen. You may lose your job, incur a disabling injury, or experience a divorce. These are unexpected changes in your life.

Or you may grow your family, own a business, or reach retirement. These expected events could also dictate a change in direction.

Your investing profile may need modification when your life changes, even in retirement. Embracing and adapting to change means asking if your allocation makes sense when interest rates go up or down or the economy expands or contracts. Every investor is different and needs the leeway to adapt to a changing investment environment.

POINTS TO REMEMBER

Your investment strategy will reflect not only your life changes but also your time horizon. This is the amount of time you have before reaching a goal. Generally, a longer time horizon means you can take greater investment risks. A shorter time horizon means striving for stability as you near financial goals.

Where do you go for advice if you're not sure how to invest? If you have a 401(k) plan and don't have enough money to pay for advice, consider blended, or balanced, funds. Most plans offer these diversified investments. They are less expensive than target date funds, which own investments based on your planned retirement date. Another alternative is an asset allocation fund, which big mutual fund companies' offer. I prefer these funds because they are more dynamic than target date funds; they typically react more quickly to economic and market changes.

Whatever investing strategy and asset allocation you choose, remember this: Life expectancies have increased dramatically over the past few decades, changing the conversation about investing. Think about your potential timeline. If you retire at sixty, you could live other twenty-five to forty years. Too much investment stability could mean instability later in life when your retirement income runs short.

WHAT INSURANCE WILL YOU NEED?

Embracing change is about more than how you invest. It's also about carrying the right amount of insurance. Salespeople will try to sell you more insurance. They may ask you to replace what you have. If you listen to more aggressive agents, you would believe that almost everyone is dramatically underinsured. I'm here to say that's not quite the case.

When you need life insurance, start by looking at the benefits your employer provides. It's sometimes free and often discounted. The same goes for disability income insurance through work. If you're young, a long-term disability from a skiing accident or knee surgery is more likely to occur than death. A younger person's ability to earn a living is everything.

Then, explore long-term care insurance. There's no need to think about it until you reach your fifties, when rates begin to rise. In most instances, I recommend that my clients with significant health problems buy this insurance in the workplace, where it's cheaper. Healthy preretirees can often do better buying a direct ownership insurance policy outside the workplace, where the market rewards their health in the form of lower premiums.

THE CROWDED WORLD OF LIFE INSURANCE

Of these three insurance products, life insurance is easily the most complex, if only because there are so many variations of it. I like term life insurance, the simplest of them, for just about anything that might happen. If you're middle-aged with lots of financial responsibilities, I believe you can justify buying a big term life policy for hundreds of thousands in death benefit. However, life insurance isn't supposed to feel like winning the lottery.

The amount of insurance you own should also change when life changes. As you pay off your mortgage and children's college costs, a small cash value, or permanent, life insurance policy is often enough. Permanent life is also a good option if you're in the highest tax bracket, because its tax-free growth is that much more valuable for higher-taxed people.

There are different types of permanent life insurance:

- **Whole life insurance.** You can own this insurance for fifty years and premiums will never increase, while the insurer issuing the policy will pay you a guaranteed rate of return.
- **Universal life insurance.** This type of permanent insurance allows you to vary the amount of premium you pay and to increase or decrease the potential death benefit. You'll get a rate of return on any cash value accumulated, adjusted annually. While this type of insurance is flexible, make sure you pay a premium high enough so the insurer can't cancel your policy.
- **Variable life insurance.** Assuming you pay your premiums on time, the previous two types of whole life insurance offer a guaranteed death benefit. Not always so with variable life insurance, where you assume much of the risk. Variable life insurance allows you to invest in stocks, bonds, and a fixed account—the insurer only guarantees the latter's rate. If you're OK with more risk in exchange for potentially higher returns, variable life might work for you.

Within these types of life insurance, there are more variations. You can invest in a portfolio mirroring a popular stock index like the Standard & Poor's as part of your universal or variable life insurance policy. You can also combine variable and universal life. Whatever you choose, a trusted financial professional or advisor can ensure you pick the right type of insurance for the changing times of your life.

CHANGE HAPPENS

In this chapter, I've offered typical scenarios that dictate specific financial actions.

Start a career, start a family, work hard, and retire. That has long been considered the typical life scenario.

The problem is there is nothing typical about Americans.

There are single people who pool their money with other singles for housing and other costs of living, but without most of the legal protections of other types of families. Their financial complications are immediate and far reaching.

There are blended families, who make up a large percentage of our population. Their change is of another magnitude, as it brings numerous and complex financial challenges.

There are same-sex couples, given equal rights that the Supreme Court upheld, but who still have financial complexities many of us can only imagine.

And there are single, older women, many of them widowed, who were in the financial dark when they were married and now must find the light and build a financial life of their own.

Everyone has a different path in his or her pursuit of life, love, and happiness. Each path has its own financial challenges and solutions.

Understand the possibilities and the probabilities. Be ready for anything. Most of all, be ready for change. Be aware of financial opportunities throughout your life. Know that financial obstacles are often temporary and that you can overcome them when you know what to expect.

Embrace change, and you will be prepared to meet any financial challenge.

Quick Guide 12: An Investment Primer for the Average Person

Maybe you are young and your only investments are in a 401(k) plan. Or maybe you have accumulated some wealth and work with an investment advisor. I've seen both types of investors make mistakes of commission and omission because they didn't know the basics of investing.

Whatever your investing skill, these eight ideas can help you avoid some mistakes:

1. **Use your scam radar.** If it sounds too good to be true, it probably is. The infamous Bernie Madoff made his investment strategies sound like they were extraordinary. He convinced otherwise successful people that if they didn't get in on his big secret, they were missing out on big money.
2. **Invest methodically.** Successful investing is boring and methodical—and it works. Invest in your employer's 401(k) plan through payroll deduction from each paycheck. Schedule automatic deductions from your checking or savings accounts to buy investments through a broker.
3. **Use time to your advantage.** Time and compounding work together like peanut butter and jam. Even if you're in your fifties, you can still put time and compounding to your advantage. After all, you could live one-third of your life in retirement
4. **Invest according to your risk tolerance.** Investing appropriately is about your risk/reward trade-off. You might have thirty years to ride out stock market ups and downs, yet hate investing mostly in stocks. Most people continue to need growth—cue stocks—in retirement because of longer lives.
5. **Diversify your investments.** We have heard this seemingly a million times: don't put all your eggs in one basket, at least when talking about your investments. Most people diversify with investments in the three major asset classes: stocks, bonds, and cash

equivalents (i.e., money market accounts), but I would add real estate in the mix, too.

True diversification means you not only mix up the asset classes you own, you also diversify according to the following factors:

- geography (e.g., domestic, international)
- economy (e.g., frontier, emerging, developed)
- industry within stocks (e.g., energy, technology)
- growth potential (e.g., growth or value stocks, high-yield or investment-grade bonds)
- bond duration (e.g., short term, long term)
- tax status (e.g., tax free bonds, taxable investments)

Diversification might also mean investing in a fourth asset class: alternatives. Investments belonging to this class include real estate, limited partnerships, and private equity. Whatever you invest in, establish an appropriate asset allocation. Then, rebalance your portfolio every few months to ensure your allocation remains true.

6. **Stay disciplined.** To invest methodically, you must stay disciplined. This is sometimes hard because you can do everything right, and many investments will still lose value over the short term, while some will lose money over the long term. I would suggest you sit tight while time helps you weather short-term fluctuations, but don't be afraid to shed long-term losers.

7. **Change when your situation changes.** Life events happen, unplanned and planned, as we progress from young adulthood through retirement. So, you must stand ready to make changes when your situation warrants it.

8. **Get professional help.** Whether you're a beginning do-it-yourself investor or an affluent person with a financial advisor, you own the responsibility to learn what you can about your investments. Ask for information. Read the prospectus. Make sure the person or company you give money to has a reputable background. Do your homework. You'll be happy you did.

Where to Learn More about Investing

Quick guide 9 at the end of chapter 3 lists a treasure trove of resources that can give you information about almost any area of personal finance. The following websites have specific information about investing for beginning to more advanced investors:

- the government agency that looks after the rights of investors, the US Securities and Exchange Commission (SEC): *www.sec.gov/ investor/pubs/begininvest.htm*
- the Financial Industry Regulatory Authority (FINRA), the industry's self-regulator: *www.finra.org/investors/types-investments*
- an SEC website for investors: *www.investor.gov/additional-resources/general-resources/publications-research/info-sheets/ 3-easy-ways-boost-your*
- from the nonprofit organization the National Endowment for Financial Education (NEFE): *www.myretirementpaycheck.org/ retirement-savings.aspx*
- another site courtesy of Uncle Sam: *www.usa.gov/saving-investing*
- and another designed especially for educators and youth: *www. mymoney.gov/save-invest/Pages/saveandinvest.aspx*

Quick Guide 13: The Fastest-Growing Type of Investment: Exchange Traded Funds

I recommend exchange traded funds (ETFs) for most of my clients because they are cheaper than mutual funds, tax-efficient, and generally inexpensive, and they are easy vehicles from which to make in-kind exchanges. Most importantly, they offer investors so much more choice than they had two decades ago.

The most basic ETFs buy investments that mirror the index tracking them. For example, you can invest in the universe of stocks through ETFs mirroring specific exchanges, such as the Standard & Poor's 500, an index of the largest publicly traded companies on US stock exchanges. Other ETFs specialize in smaller companies, domestic companies, and foreign ones, and specific sectors, including technology and energy.

ETFs are also common in the fixed-income world, where they invest in US bonds and notes, corporate bonds, and municipal bonds. They can also hold commodities like gold, silver, and coffee, as well as currency from around the world and real estate.

The more basic the ETF, the lower the fees and expenses—as low as 0.045 percent compared to enhanced ETF costs, which range from 1 to 2 percent on up. Enhanced ETFs are "active" investments, meaning asset managers analyze holdings as they do with mutual funds. Enhanced ETF managers can bet on market booms, busts, and particular sectors, like financial services, or parts of sectors like banks.

Your rule of thumb when investing in ETFs is that the more one varies from the index it supposedly tracks, the more it will cost you in fees and expenses. Because average to high mutual fund fees can have an outsized effect on how well a portfolio's investments perform, I like low-cost ETFs as a way to meet a variety of my clients' investing goals.

Quick Guide 14: Life Stages and Their Financial Challenges

Whether a financial earthquake is your motivation for learning more about managing your money or you have a burning desire to acquire and build on sound money skills, you will run into obstacles throughout the stages of your life. The following tips can help guide you through some challenges.

NEW ADULT

1. **Be realistic about how much college debt you can owe.** Few majors are worth the obscene amount of debt some students carry. Consider the entry-level and subsequent salary levels of a chosen career. Know that if you're like most people, you will change careers often, requiring additional education.
2. **An ATM card is not free money.** Your bank will deduct withdrawals from your checking account.
3. **Your new credit card is also not free money.** You must pay it all back at some point—with interest. Making minimum payments is a surefire recipe to staying in debt forever.
4. **Keep records.** Don't assume your checkbook will balance itself.

COLLEGE GRADUATE

1. **Consider living at home after college to save money.** Even if you're single, you might want to save for a future wedding, first home, and additional education. Mom and dad can help, especially if they charge little or no rent. (You might also want to get your parents to buy into the idea!) Understand that *temporary* means your living arrangement has an expiration date.
2. **Carefully weigh paying off college debt versus credit card debt.** Other than introductory offers, credit cards have higher interest rates than college loans do.

NEWLYWEDS

1. **Consider how to merge your finances.** This can be tricky, especially if one spouse is a saver and the other a spender. Keep some money in joint accounts, but maintain your individual financial identity with a separate account, especially if you're a woman.
2. **Establish ceilings for what you will spend on certain items.** This means looking only at houses listed at $300,000 if that is your limit. This means looking only at cars that, with options, are within your fixed limit. Put price ceilings on restaurant meals, major appliances, and more.

YOUNG FAMILIES

1. **Once you have children, everything changes.** They are now the center of your life, and you want to give them everything. Ask yourself if they really need more outfits than days in a month or every toy and game advertised on television. Resist!
2. **Consider the true cost of both parents working when your kids are young.** What's the true cost of one parent staying at home, now and in the future? Step back and look at your top priorities, financial and otherwise. There are no right or wrong answers. But like every financial decision you make, one choice will affect your other decisions.
3. **Spend smartly on school.** I know people who paid dearly to put their kids in private grammar school and high school, only to regret they didn't put the money toward escalating college costs. Consider a town's reputation for public education when buying a house. Know that college will *not* cost less in the future.
4. **Continue the practice of establishing ceilings on what you will spend.** You can blow your budget for a week at Disney World with kids who aren't old enough to appreciate the characters. Or you can plan vacations with a budget in mind. Know that one

week at the shore or lake that is only a car ride away will create a memory just as lasting as the most expensive vacation.

5. **Weigh *needs* and *wants*.** It's easy for McMansions to lure some of us into thinking we need bigger homes. If you're already comfortable, why bother? Keep building the equity on your first home. Build an extension if this is a more cost-efficient solution for a growing family.

MATURING FAMILIES

1. **As kids grow older, your income *could* grow because you could pay more attention to career prospects.** Invest in your career if it makes sense. It made sense for me, for example, to earn a Certified Investment Management Analyst certification as my career progressed.

2. **College costs are getting real at this point.** Do you save for your kids' college or take an expensive family vacation? The trade-offs seem like one-off decisions, but they are not. Everything affects everything else.

3. **Think hard about taking on a ton of debt for your children's college costs.** That's because you could be paying this bill well into retirement, and...

4. **Retirement is not as far off as before.** Where did the last twenty years go? What have you done so far to prepare for retirement? If you've done nothing, thankfully you still have time to prepare.

EMPTY NESTERS

1. **With so much talk about boomerang kids—those who graduate college and return home to live—you might think families never go their separate ways.** They do. And when it happens, you should take advantage by saving more money.

2. **Consider reducing your life insurance coverage if you expect to earn less in retirement than today.** This is also true if you have a lot of home equity, your kids are doing well on their own, your parents don't need you to care for them, and other financial obligations are light.

3. **As you near retirement, consider working with a financial professional—if you're not already—to ensure your investment mix is right for your life stage.**

4. **Communicate with your parents.** Odds are they may need some long-term care sooner or later, and you'll want to know their expectations and capability of paying for it.

5. **Reduce your debt.** The amount of debt you owe in retirement will directly affect how long your funds will last. Few investments' returns can match what you pay in interest for the average credit card.

RETIREES

1. **This isn't your parents' retirement.** At sixty-five, you may keep working, work part time, or start a business. Hopefully, you have prepared well enough, and a lack of funds doesn't drive your decision.

2. **Make sure you are financially equipped to handle potential long-term care costs for you and your spouse.** A separate fund, insurance, and family may provide full or partial solutions.

3. **You won't be traveling around the world when you reach one hundred.** The truth is that we do the majority of our traveling before we reach seventy-five, and then expenses and travel drop off sharply after that.

4. **Put your final plans into writing.** In the next chapter, we'll talk more about these and other documents you should consider having.

Seven

Habit 6: Use the Right Resources at the Right Time

A s an amateur triathlete, I spend a lot of my spare time riding my bicycle in the towns near mine. I actually like to get lost and find my way back. My racing buddies and I call this KT's great adventures.

The goal of the ride is to log some miles and have some fun, not to get from point A to B in the straightest possible line. Sometimes it's fun to say, "I want to go where this road leads."

That is seldom true, though, when it comes to money. Sure, there is a point in your life when you have both the time and the desire to figure money things out. However, there comes a point when all of us can benefit from some timely advice.

While embracing change can help you meet various financial concerns throughout your life, successfully dealing with change requires preparation and a willingness to use the right resources at the right time.

I'm a firm believer that, while you may be living a different stage of life than the person next to you, the need for qualified help to navigate around financial obstacles is common to everyone. Qualified help includes everything from faceless online resources to specialists who spend countless hours perfecting their crafts and reaching the top of their professions.

Here's a look at different ways to use the right resources at the right time.

DO IT YOURSELF—WITH CAUTION

In today's connected world, you can find information on just about every topic. Finding authoritative information is another story. You'll have to dig to find reputable sources if you do your research online.

Crowdsourcing is one way to find a resource for nonfinancial matters. Think about your own life. You might go to one website to get a restaurant review, another for an electrician, and a third to learn more about a doctor or hospital. Crowdsourcing is a way of getting firsthand advice. The idea is that the more opinions you get, the better the advice. A word of warning, though: just because it's on Twitter or Facebook doesn't make it true.

Put another way, free information is free only when it doesn't result in a poor decision that costs you in the end.

MONITOR YOUR CREDIT

Veracity is crucial when you need to find answers about financial subjects. With less complicated subjects like credit, you can find the info you need at no cost other than the time you put into it. For example, you can monitor your own credit and save the ten to fifty dollars per month some credit monitoring companies charge to do it for you.

You might also monitor your online checking, savings, and investment accounts regularly for unusual activity. Most financial institutions are liable for fraudulent withdrawals as long you notify them in a timely way. Looking at your checking account monthly or monitoring your credit card charges every three months is not timely, so take a few extra minutes every few days to check your accounts.

Check your credit report regularly. Federal law allows you to get a free copy of your credit report every twelve months from each of the three major credit reporting companies: Equifax, Experian, and TransUnion. You can get your free copy at www.annualcreditreport. com. The law also gives you the right to a free report if a company denies you credit, insurance, or employment within the same twelve months. You must request your credit report within sixty days of receiving notice of denial.

ONLINE CALCULATORS

Doing it yourself may suffice in other areas of your financial life, too. For example, you can compare term insurance premiums online. If you want to buy term life insurance, first determine how much you really need. Some sites will suggest you need higher amounts than necessary.

A website like NerdWallet (www.nerdwallet.com) has online calculators that help you determine a reasonable amount of life insurance to carry. This and other sites like SelectQuote (www.selectquote.com) and QuickQuote (www.quickquote.com) will compare rates of the different companies' term insurance products. Find a qualified financial professional who can help if you have less basic questions such as what type of life insurance to buy.

Wherever you turn online, a variety of online calculators can help you figure out everything from how much mortgage you can afford to the best credit card rates. You can also shop around on reputable financial websites for the best auto insurance, used car prices and loans, and mortgage rates.

Generic consumer websites are useful, but smartphone applications and Internet bots that provide quick, simple financial answers can also help you. Websites and applications from your company 401(k) plan and health insurance providers will provide more specific information, too.

Every Generation Is Different

Baby boomers may have changed everything they touched (and continue to touch in retirement), but millennials take their own path as they travel into and through adulthood. They listen to Bloomberg and watch CNBC. They use robo-advisors like Betterment™, E*TRADE®, and Wealthfront, or they do their own research and invest on their own.

Whatever the task, they like to do most things themselves, and sometimes things don't work out. However, Baby boomers weren't any better at figuring out finances when they were young than millennials are now. In fact, today's youngest adults are cost-sensitive and better consumers because they must be in a more complicated world.

So, millennials don't want to pay fees for checking. Are they wrong? They generally don't own homes yet because they don't want to spend more than they earn. They tend to pay for value, and that's a motto we can all live by.

Employee benefits plans, in fact, often include most of the financial products Americans own. Employers are on the front lines of many Americans' financial wellness attempts, so don't hesitate to use the financial resources they provide. They are the right resources at the right time.

While you may have an endless supply of resources to help you with just about any subject, remember again that free isn't free if bad information steers you to an inferior financial outcome. Your task, should you choose to accept it, is to find good advice in the most appropriate form. This task shouldn't be mission impossible for anyone.

NEXT LEVEL OF SERVICE

As you age, increase your family size, and watch your financial situation become more complicated, it's natural to seek professional advice. This comes in many shapes and forms.

You may need legal advice at some point in your life, if only to draw up a will. The American Bar Association has a referral process that can help you choose an attorney from a variety of specialties.

Many people hire accountants as their taxes become more complicated. You can hire a simple tax preparer—know that you can become one with just a few hours of study—or work with a certified public accountant (CPA), depending on your tax complexity. You can locate a CPA by finding your state CPA organization's contact information on the American Institute of CPAs website.

You may also decide it's time to look for a financial advisor. Or one will find you, especially if you are relatively affluent. Just know that there are no rules governing the term *financial advisor*. Most advisors are well intentioned, but good intentions don't necessarily guarantee expertise.

When it's time to look for a financial advisor, know that you are responsible for doing your homework to ensure a proper choice. Always remember that if it seems too good to be true, it probably is.

WHEN COMPLEX FINANCES REQUIRE ESTATE PLANNING

Depending on your financial complexity, you may need other professionals to help you along life's many paths. For many people, a will, power of attorney, and a healthcare directive are enough (see quick guide 19). Others care for aging parents, have children from a first marriage, or are one-half of a same-sex union. These and other family situations prove there is more to estate planning than money.

FAMILIES WITH AGING PARENTS

As you age, for example, it's hard to know when it's time to bring someone in to help you. Now I know people are funny about money, especially when it comes to sharing financial information with their kids. I understand the reluctance to address this issue. After all, who wants to relinquish control? You want to be in charge and keep your independence. Still, older kids belong in this conversation.

I believe lack of communication leads to the elder shame issue, when older Americans begin taking financial and other missteps because they didn't plan for a cognitive or physical decline. This can happen to anyone. Take driving, for instance, as one issue that can create sparks. I have seen tensions rise when adult children tell their parents they shouldn't drive anymore. The roles have reversed. Parents now feel like children, and their children are acting like their parents. The kids are telling mom and dad what they should do, but mom and dad don't want to give up their independence.

Before you get to that impasse, talk it out. You need to trust and really listen to somebody, whether that person is family or a longtime financial or legal advisor. The scariest words I hear from clients are "whatever you say, Kathleen." It's nice to have trust, but it also could mean they don't understand what I'm saying and won't follow through. This is scary, because lack of action creates an incubator in which senior fraud occurs.

Long-term care is another hush-hush subject that shouldn't be so. Once upon a time, you could give money to family and charities to bankrupt yourself and thus receive government-subsidized long-term care from Medicaid. Today, rules have tightened, and assets given away within a certain time frame before you need long-term care are included among your total assets, potentially eliminating the free or cheaper care.

There are other strategies you can use to limit long-term care costs. Because these rules change all the time, you might consider engaging an elder law attorney before doing anything. With planning, you would know what to do and how to prepare for long-term care and other eventualities.

For example, learn if it is in your best interest to choose someone to act on your behalf as an executor of a will or a trustee of a trust. If so, when? Think about it when you're in your early to mid-seventies. If your estate is simple, a child might serve as executor. If your estate is more complex, you might think about professional advice. At this age, you might already be paying advisors for this counsel, so use their expertise. As you need more planning, they'll do more. That's what you pay us financial advisors to do.

Whatever you do for whatever your situation is, talk it out. Communication is the first step.

MARRIED COUPLES

Laws today are structured with married people in mind. The traditional, long-term married couple with no children from former marriages tends to have a more simplified estate plan. As the writing of this book, there is no limit on the amount of money one spouse can give or will to their legal spouse. If you have children, you might worry about potential taxes and expenses to get these funds to your children or seeing your assets reduced by a potential long-term care risk. But for the most part, the planning seems to be fairly straightforward. However, for the rest of us, there can definitely be some twists.

BLENDED FAMILIES

According to the US Census Bureau's American Community Survey, 17 percent of Americans have married at least twice. This creates potential estate planning nightmares, especially for blended families with children from a previous marriage.

I caution my clients in this situation. There are often hard feelings when the estate plan doesn't take children from a blended family into account. Stepchildren clearly resent the idea that they must wait for the death of a stepparent to receive any assets from their own parent. Often, these children are written out from their biological parent because the assets go outright to the new spouse, and then later, the spouse either re-marries or has only their biological children as beneficiaries of the estate.

How do you protect assets for children from your first marriage, especially when probate courts might favor the current spouse and family of the deceased? An estate planning attorney might recommend something like a QTIP trust, which ensures some income for the surviving spouse and return of some assets to children from a previous marriage once the spouse passes.

SPECIAL-NEEDS CHILDREN

Families who must provide for the lifetime needs of a disabled child face unique challenges, not the least being financial. A special-needs trust permits them to set aside some money for a child's needs without forfeiting Medicare benefits. Relatively cash-poor, special-needs children can lose federal benefits when their assets exceed low levels, which is why you should get the help of an attorney experienced in this area. There are more than a few rules for creating and using these trusts, so make sure not to run afoul of them. If you do, the federal government can claw back money it paid for care.

LIFELONG SINGLES

You might think committed single people wouldn't have an estate planning care in the world, but they do. One concern revolves around where to live as they get older and how to access help when needed.

I find that single people are more apt to live in a community housing environment, including condominiums and apartment buildings, than in a large home. Single people typically live in cities rather than out in the woods. Wherever they reside, they must plan for eventual care and its cost. Singles living by themselves should also ask who would take care of them when they are sick or, over the longer term, disabled. Like married couples, singles should compare the cost and availability of long-term care insurance and their ability to pay someone out of pocket to care for them at home.

If you're single and you need serious care, will you have the assets or insurance needed to pay a care facility, or will you spend down your assets to qualify for Medicare or Medicaid, which will then pay for care? Keep in mind the federal government has claw back provisions for single people, too.

Singles, of course, will have other financial challenges. Because default beneficiaries might not be obvious, a will is a necessary first estate planning step. If a single person wants to leave a financial legacy to a sibling, nephew, or niece, life insurance may be the appropriate choice because beneficiaries receive the benefit income-tax-free. Being single doesn't mean you don't have someone you care for.

UNMARRIED AND SAME-SEX COUPLES

Despite legal advances, same-sex couples face unique financial challenges from life through death. The Supreme Court may have OK'd same-sex marriage, but if state law doesn't follow suit, estate chaos can ensue.

First, same-sex couples should take some steps that help all my clients. Bank accounts, investment accounts, and insurance policies with up-to-date beneficiary designations help ensure the orderly transfer of assets. For any couple living together without marriage, wills are essential, and while estate planning isn't an absolute necessity, it almost. Without a will and a marriage license, the courts will distribute assets to blood relatives instead of to an unmarried life partner.

Still, despite potential legal difficulties of not marrying and recent gains in marriage rights, same-sex couples aren't rushing to the altar. Generally, young adults aren't either. Instead, more couples are living together and passing on marriage—in part, to avoid entangling their finances.

Even community property laws may not help when couples are not legally married. While some states have these community property laws that address couples who live together a certain number of years, these laws might not help you distribute assets properly. Here's why:

First, this is a nuanced side of the marketplace, and if you are not married, you are not legally protected under the law like a legally married person. Second, most states don't have community property laws. If you live with someone in one of these states and you're not married, you have no rights of ownership if you split—unless you have an updated and signed will, trusts, or other planning documents in place.

Today, marriage is on the decline. Millennials either aren't marrying or will marry later. When you don't have marriage rights, planning takes on added importance. This may require only a beneficiary change on investments and life insurance. Or it may require a change in property ownership on a deed. Whatever your living arrangement, make sure you take the necessary steps to protect yourself and loved ones financially.

ADVICE APPROPRIATE FOR YOU

Whatever your living situation may be, you must find the right resource at the right time that is appropriate to your situation. Consider the costs of doing it yourself versus getting the help of a professional. Many people buy tax software and then spend three weekends working on it to save $150. Is that a good deal? It depends on how much you value your time.

On the other hand, maybe you don't need to see an attorney for basic legal advice, like how to draw up a will, when an online service like LegalZoom might suffice. If you have more complex legal issues, then by all means, see an estate planning attorney.

Millennials just entering the workforce can invest through their employers and compare insurance rates online without the need for an advisor. If you're a new homeowner just beginning a family, you might consider a robo-advisor for investments and a tax preparer to do your taxes.

Then again, you don't know what you don't know, and you may need advice from a real, live, qualified financial professional. A newly married couple may not understand how to manage combined finances. Parents may be confused about saving for college, retirement, or both. Tying all of this together usually requires a real person or persons.

The more complex your financial situation is, the greater your potential need for financial, legal, and accounting advice. Ultimately, the solutions you find online or in person are only as good as the sources providing them. As always, do your homework to make an informed decision, and use the right resources at the right time.

Quick Guide 15: When Should You Choose a Financial Advisor?

I can think of five good reasons to consider working with a professional financial advisor.

1. **When you plan to put all your financial information into Quicken, but don't.**
2. **When you repeat the same New Year's resolution about getting your finances in order.**
3. **When you can't figure out what you own in your company 401(k) plan.**
4. **When you see growth in your income and net worth but shrinkage in the time you must care for them.**
5. **When you don't know what you don't know.**
6. **Does this sound familiar to you?**

WHAT'S IN A NAME?

One of problems with the financial advice industry is that virtually everyone can call themselves a financial advisor or a financial planner. Look for the right credentials. One is CFP, an acronym for *certified financial planner*. CFPs must complete comprehensive financial education, pass a tough exam, abide by a strict code of ethics, and continue their education. A CFP has studied investment management, portfolio analysis, estate planning, retirement planning, insurance, and taxes.

The Master of Science in Financial Services (MSFS), granted by the American College, is another designation signifying financial knowledge and ethics. A third is the Certified Investment Management Analyst (CIMA), a designation concentrating on investing. I'm proud that I was one of a small percentage of women to earn this latter designation.

These three are among the handful of financial advisor designations that require serious study and a commitment to putting clients first. Learn more about literally more than one hundred financial designations and what's involved with earning each via the Financial Industry Regulatory Authority (FINRA), the self-regulatory body governing investment advisors. Know that not all designations are the same, and some require little to no effort to gain.

TRUST, BUT VERIFY

Once you find advisor candidates, check them for past violations. Most states have financial services departments that keep track of complaints and actions taken against advisors. FINRA also keeps a history of actions against its membership at www.brokercheck.org.

UNDERSTAND YOUR COSTS

Before choosing an advisor, decide how to pay for an advisor's services. My take on fees is that if you don't understand what you're paying or why, you're paying too much. And if your advice costs nothing, you should be skeptical. There is no free lunch in the financial world.

Understanding how some advisors are paid can seem surreal. You have fee-based, commission-based, and hourly based advisors, and there's much more that might be hidden from you. Advisors could receive asset management fees for managing your money or for bundling financial products with one provider.

Insurance and annuity providers typically pay agents and advisors up front, with the cost hidden in the price of the product. That's not even including surrender charges, which annuity owners typically must pay if they give up their annuity during the first seven to ten years of its contract.

How much should *you* pay? Consider an hourly arrangement if you have one-time financial advice needs like how to pay down credit cards versus paying down a mortgage. Maybe an hourly agreement works if you only need asset allocation advice about retirement investing in accounts not with an advisor or about whether to exercise stock options.

For asset management and investment products, you'll find three types of compensation. The first is *commission based*. This is an incentive for advisors to place your investments with the company paying commissions, but it is little if any incentive for them to help you manage the investment.

Fee-based advisors charge a fee as a percentage of assets managed, but they can still take commissions for selling insurance and other financial services.

A *fee-only* advisor charges an annual percentage fee for managing assets and an hourly or set fee for specific one-time advice or periodic services like financial planning.

ON THE SAME SIDE

A fee-only advisor means just that—*only*! I am a fee-only advisor, ensuring that I stay on the same side of the table as my clients. I charge my clients a fee for services, but I don't take commissions or make money in other ways.

Advisory fees often range from less than 1 percent to more than 2 percent, depending on what you have and need. In recent years, the cost of investments has declined, but if your advisor hasn't shared these savings with you, find out why.

OTHER COSTS

Investors should become familiar with other costs that can detract from their return. Trailing commissions from mutual funds provide additional income for advisory firms and their advisors. Funds also charge marketing and other expenses, which is why you should always look at an investment's net return, not its total return. Index and exchange traded funds are good at keeping expenses low in general, but it's always important to understand what you are paying.

Bonds are the most subjective investment to purchase because the true cost is buried in the purchase price, while the broker's commission is not stated. People with direct bond ownership should ask their brokers specifically about how much they are paid in commissions.

Some advisors pass on trading costs to clients. This can total hundreds of dollars per year in the form of increased total expenses that reduce potential returns. I don't do this. Again, know all your costs, and make sure managing investment expenses is part of your advisor's mandate.

Ultimately, no matter how your financial advisor is paid, learn all you can about charges, fees, and expenses. The more you pay, the lower your potential net return on investments will be.

Quick Guide 16: Three Estate Planning Documents Almost Everyone Needs

Financial planning is about more than growing and preserving your assets; it's about putting safeguards in place so we and our loved ones can deal with life's big decisions. The following three legal documents can help you establish safeguards.

WILL

A will is a legal document that spells out in writing your final wishes. No one can predict the future, which is why anyone with any assets or loved ones should have a will. If you don't put your wishes in writing to establish who gets your assets, a probate court might decide for you.

Understand that despite its legal standing, a will is only as good as the information in it. My favorite fact about wills is that they reflect your plans right now, but you can change them as your plans change. Want to leave money to your grandkids directly? Write it in. They decide to travel as followers of a rock band, write them out! It's your choice.

On a more serious note, a will should dictate more than a transfer of assets. If you care for dependent kids, special-needs adult children, or cognitively impaired parents, name their guardians and terms of their care in your will.

LIVING TRUST

The terms of any will become public in probate court, which could be problematic for those who don't want their financial affairs made public, like a business owner who doesn't want the competition to gain an unfair advantage. A living trust helps you avoid the public glare of probate, allows you to build a more complex distribution list, and could potentially help you avoid estate taxes.

Like a will, living trusts are revocable—you can change their terms at any time. (There are more complex trusts that are irrevocable, which you should enter into only with the help of an estate planning attorney.)

A living will can also help get your assets distributed more quickly than typical probate court proceedings allow.

POWERS OF ATTORNEY

In addition to a living trust or will, you might consider drawing up powers of attorney. There are two types: financial and healthcare. A financial power of attorney names a person, usually a loved one, to manage your financial affairs if you can't. The reasons you might grant such powers include an extended period out of the country or an incapacitation.

You can establish durable powers of attorney, which grant these powers when conditions dictate them over time, or ordinary powers, which are for a specific timeframe.

HEALTHCARE DIRECTIVE

A healthcare directive, sometimes known as a living will or healthcare power of attorney, also grants power to a person to make decisions for you—this time about your healthcare matters—when you are too incapacitated to do so yourself. You can state in this legal document the types of medical treatment you are willing to receive (and not receive), as well as whether you want life support if needed.

Disclaimer: This information does not constitute legal advice. Please contact an attorney to learn more about these and other important legal documents.

Quick Guide #17: Prenuptial Agreements Are for Almost Everyone

If you're married, I'll bet your first reaction to this headline was to say, "Not me!"

I've heard it all before, the not-me's echoing in my head even today when I recommend prenuptial agreements to clients. I've also seen despair when head-over-heels love deteriorates into something less than that—and to divorce—taking with it some of the wealth one person had coming into the marriage.

Movies have given prenuptial agreements a bad rap. If you enter a marriage with wealth, it's important to look at this planning tool. A prenup directs how to distribute assets if a marriage fails. It can be complicated or simple, but some rules apply to them all. Fail to follow these rules, and it can void the agreement.

First, everyone must disclose everything.

That's *everyone*.

And *everything*.

The single biggest reason I've seen prenups voided in court is because one partner refused to divulge *all* financial assets. I had one client who refused because she thought if she disclosed all her wealth, her fiancé would never sign the agreement. So, compounding what was probably a wrong impression, she didn't disclose every asset. You can guess the end of this story. The marriage failed after a couple of years, and a good portion of her assets became his.

Before creating a prenup, find out how your state handles one. A competent attorney should be able to answer any questions, but the burden is on you to find out everything you can. I've had clients in second marriages mess up their estate planning because they didn't update their wills. Massachusetts, for instance, is good at making the simple complex when it comes to prenups and wills.

I've also seen clients who wouldn't entertain even the thought of a prenuptial agreement because they believed that love conquered all. My experience described earlier in this book proved that love is not always eternal. Fortunately, I was young and still making my way in the world. However, this status didn't ease the pain when my ex went his separate way with what few assets I had.

Legally Separating Matters

Let's face it, divorce happens. And if it happens to you, pay attention to your assets. Don't assume your spouse would never take your assets. This assumption is risky. You can avoid financial surprises by legally separating before a divorce.

Sadly, this is a step many skip, but you skip it at your own demise.

A legal separation dictates child support and custody for an interim period. It also provides a legal accounting of who owns what, both individually and jointly. If assets you own disappear, a legal separation allows you to recoup assets of yours as an offset to an eventual divorce settlement.

A legal separation is a legally enforceable agreement, so work with a qualified divorce attorney before entering one.

Widows and widowers are particularly vulnerable to "prenup-itis" because they tend to avoid uncomfortable conversations with future partners. Knowing this, I deliver this message to every widow and widower who is a client of mine:

I know you are not thinking about this right now, but the day will come where you might start thinking seriously about someone new. Now is also the time to consider a prenuptial agreement. You are young. You may meet someone else. Because you experienced marriage that was till death do us part, you probably want to discount the importance of this agreement.

You and your first spouse worked hard for your assets. These assets are likely the floor that will provide stability to you and your children for years to come. But if you have assets that you thought would go to your children someday and you fail to segregate these assets, you just made *your* assets a marital asset.

When you feel yourself getting serious about someone, we should talk about how a prenup can protect you and your children. Then, if you enter another serious relationship and are ready to talk, we can discuss how to have the conversation with a new partner. My recommendation is early and often. Let your future partner know this is important to you. You might find it's important to your new partner, too.

It comes down to this: Prenups don't have to be eternal. In my mind, you're either married or you're not after a certain period of time, say seven years. But I am a proponent of prenuptial agreements for clients entering a marriage where assets are uneven, and especially when there are children not shared in the marriage. Just know this agreement doesn't have to be a forever document. As with everything else financial, do your homework before making any decisions.

Eight

Habit 7: It All Comes Down to Income Planning

A daptive distribution theory, which is the opposite of choosing a withdrawal rate and sticking with it, addresses the ebbs and flows of retirement. Instead of taking 4 percent or 5 percent every single year, the theory suggests that you withdraw *what you really need when you need it*.

OUR LIVES AREN'T STATIC

I recommend my clients start retirement with a 4.5–5.5 percent withdrawal rate. This way, they meet their income requirements when they're highest—early in retirement—without risking running out of money in the future. We also might increase the withdrawal rate to match inflation. Here, I look at an individual's inflation rate, not a government-issued number. If you don't increase your withdrawals when car insurance premiums, property taxes, and healthcare expenses increase, you'll have less money to spend for life's other needs and wants.

Now maybe you can make up some of the shortfall by cutting costs elsewhere. If apples increase in price and oranges don't, eat the less expensive fruit. Or maybe you need to increase your withdrawals because you can't eat oranges. Retirees duplicate this tongue-in-cheek example in more serious ways every day. This is how we live.

We take more from our retirement accounts because of one-off expenses like a new car or paying for a child's wedding. But we don't write this rule into stone. If the stock market behaves badly, maybe you wait an extra year or two to buy that car. Your withdrawal program should be flexible to deal with financial surprises and to acknowledge that if you're like most retirees, you'll eventually slow down and spend less. When your needs change, your withdrawal strategy should change accordingly.

ESTABLISH *NEEDS* AND *WANTS*

I urge my clients to begin income planning two to five years before they retire. Start by separating your anticipated spending into two buckets: *needs* and *wants*. If you remember in chapter 4, we talked about this bucket approach as methodology that becomes more important as we age.

You need to keep the lights on. You need to eat and to pay for healthcare and other necessities. That's one bucket.

You want to eat out more often. You want to take nicer and more frequent vacations. That's another bucket where your disposable retirement income might go. When times are tough, you can put off your wants but not your needs.

Once needs and wants are established, I tell my clients they can't use a cookie cutter approach to figure out their retirement withdrawals. The right retirement income strategy will address both good economic times and bad. The text box provides one example of how this might work.

ONE RETIREMENT INCOME STRATEGY

- Start with $500,000 in retirement savings.
- Begin with a 5% withdrawal rate, adjusted for personal inflation and spending.

- Figure $18,000 annually, or $1,500 per month, will pay for your needs.
- Take another $7,000 a year for a new car down payment, vacations, and other discretionary expenses.
- Reduce the last number when markets falter or unexpected expenses occur.
- Keep investing for some growth, so that you add to your savings.

INCOME NEEDS WON'T REMAIN STATIC

Our lives ebb and flow like the waves that hit the shores of the ocean. Nowhere is this more apparent than in our later years. You might battle multiple chronic health conditions throughout your life or be the picture of health, but we all will slow down to varying extents as we age. The withdrawal strategy that meets your financial needs in retirement adapts to changes in your life.

I can't take credit for the commonsense approach. James Sandidge, author of *Risk, Psychology and Retirement Income: Why Conventional Wisdom Is Wrong about Wealth Distribution and What the Research Really Shows*, wrote a paper on adaptive distribution theory, first published in the *Journal of Investment Consulting*. In his paper, Sandidge used statistics from the Employee Benefit Research Institute that showed spending decreased between age fifty and eighty-nine for people of all financial means. He emphasized the need to manage risk and cash flow rather than follow an autopilot-type of approach.

I couldn't agree more.

Once you establish needs and wants, take a good look at where you'll get your income. It could come from a retirement plan like a pension, 401(k) plan, or IRA. It might come from individual investments, real estate income, or part-time work.

Serial Roth Conversion

When I talk to clients about how to gradually convert taxable retirement money to a Roth IRA, I explain that every person gets thousands of dollars income-tax-free, courtesy of our tax code, before taxes kick in. From 0%, the graduated tax rate climbs to 10%, 15%, and 25% brackets, before rising to 28%, 33%, and finally 36%. The idea behind the Roth conversion strategy is to burn through the lower brackets by converting taxable retirement income to a Roth when your income and tax rate are lowest.

Here's an example. Let's say you and your spouse need $70,000 annually in income. Federal income taxes don't rise above 15% for a couple in tax year 2016 until they exceed $75,900 jointly, after subtracting deductions and exemptions.

So, you start by counting on $30,000 from Social Security. Now you need $40,000 from your retirement accounts. This $70,000 in gross income is closer to $50,000 net after deductions and exemptions. Now you have almost $26,000 to spare before triggering the next tax rate of 25% for adjusted gross incomes of $75,900 and more. Converting $26,000 at a 15% tax rate means you pay $3,900 extra in taxes. That's for $26,000 of now-and-forever tax-free retirement income in the Roth!

Tax planning isn't paying the least in any single year, but paying the least over your lifetime. People miss this point because they cannot change a lifetime of programming that says deferral is best, even though this is not true when compared to cheaper and free.

ROTH IRA DIFFERENCE

As I wrote previously, the Roth IRA is the only other truly tax-free investment retirement savings vehicle. I believe this is the only way to own something that is both tax-free and offers growth potential. Taxes can be huge part of your expenses in retirement, and a Roth IRA can help alleviate some of this concern. If you already have a Roth IRA, you know that your contributions were not tax deductible. Everything else, including investment gains, is tax-free. There's nothing else like it.

If you don't have a Roth IRA, consider converting a traditional IRA—which is fully or partially taxable—to a Roth. The IRS and possibly your state will expect its share of taxes on the amount you convert, but the advantage of converting is that future investment gains and all withdrawals will be tax-free.

WHAT WILL YOUR RETIREMENT LOOK LIKE?

You may have multiple retirement investment strategies, but your solution almost always comes down to the answer to this simple question: How much money will make you comfortable? This requires a full awareness of what you want out of life and what you're willing to give in return for it.

Some people will live modestly and take what their investments and the economy bring. Others want more and take steps to get there. Income plan accordingly. My happiest retirees have no mortgage, little debt, and some guaranteed income through pensions, annuities, or real estate. They tend to follow a strategy that recognizes markets have poor stretches. They know inflation can reduce real dollars.

They might even continue working. It's always nicer to make a major decision like working when you reach retirement age because you want to, not because you have to. Many encore careerists happily return to work to bring in extra income and the added comfort it brings. This isn't unusual. Baby Boomers in the 55–64-year-old age bracket made up 24.3 percent of all new business owners in 2015, a significant jump from the 14.8 percent of new business owners in that age group in 1996. Baby boomers have always done things differently, including becoming late-in-life business owners.

Longer lives, however, are new. As a group, baby boomers will live longer than past generations of Americans, meaning retirement can last thirty or more years. My clients realize there's only so much golf they can play. Some people, me included, decide that work is another way to keep busy.

It's funny how retirement plans change. When I was forty-five, I talked about early retirement. At fifty-two, I talked about working a little longer. I'm guessing that when I'm sixty-four, I may be ready to retire. But who knows?

The prospect of staying retired for decades is daunting, and I see people working longer because of this. I have a ninety-year-old client, living independently, who said to me, "Can you imagine I've been retired as long as I worked?" This is a probability for many people, not a possibility, and it makes people less anxious to retire.

WHAT WILL YOUR RETIREMENT LOOK LIKE?

Whether you continue to work or not during your "retirement" years, try to envision what this stage of your life will look like. First, understand that your income stream will experience disruptions. For example, wanting to own a business—if that's what you choose—won't make it successful. Know your chances of creating a going concern versus financing an expensive hobby if you choose this path.

Second, understand that investment gains in your retirement accounts will not be constant. There will be times when the market falters and your investment income wanes.

Third, know that you'll breathe easier with a little bit of financial cushion. This doesn't mean making outrageous projections of your life expectancy and investment gains, but making continuous risk management of your investment portfolio a regular task. Realize you will need more than a little cushion, for instance, if you invest in near-zero-interest fixed income investments.

Fourth, make sure you understand these and other facets of your income stream, including Social Security payments, rental income, and other pension and retirement plan income.

Finally, know for certain that regardless of trends in which baby boomers are taking on new mortgages and other financial commitments, debt will not be your friend in retirement. You must manage debt wisely as part of a comprehensive financial strategy.

So, if you're among the growing number of people with a child's college debt on your tab as you approach retirement, consider paying this off a top priority—or plan to delay your retirement.

THE SHIFT FROM SAVING TO SPENDING

If you take these and other steps and you can retire with certainty and comfort, you will have one more task that is more difficult than you might expect: the shift from saving to spending. This is especially true for investors who were obsessive about saving enough for retirement.

This difficulty in shifting to a spending mind-set brings me back to James Sandidge's adaptive distribution theory. If you deprive yourself in retirement because you can't rid yourself of an ingrained obsession to save enough to last a lifetime, remember that you will likely spend less money as you age.

Think about this shift another way: If you were insistent on saving for retirement in a disciplined way, there must have been a reason for this, right? Longer vacations, more meals out, more time with the grandkids, and more money for favorite charities may have been your impetus to save. You saved what you wanted to save, and you've taken steps to manage your income flow realistically.

One of those steps many of my retired clients take to manage their income flow is to devote around half of their portfolio to growth investments. This doesn't necessarily mean taking on huge risk for big reward, but it can include investments in dividend-paying stock, real estate, and index funds featuring large companies. I realize, however, that some investors have little appetite for any risk, so I adjust my recommendations accordingly.

Once you have done all the hard work, pat yourself on the back and congratulate yourself. Now do the only thing you have left to do: begin spending.

Remember why you diligently saved. Ignore the television commercials and social media warnings about the possibility of living to one hundred, because you've considered everything as part of your strategy, and even if you do live to be one hundred, you probably won't spend as you do now. Sometimes you will turn the money faucet higher and other times lower to account for what's happening at specific times in your life.

You reached your finish line. Enjoy what you worked a lifetime to achieve.

Quick Guide #18: The Ins and Outs of Retirement Income

We think about taxes a lot when we invest. While you saved or continue saving for retirement, you probably put a lot of your retirement savings into tax-qualified accounts or plans. The term *qualified* signifies tax-advantaged investing. The Internal Revenue Service (IRS) lets taxpayers defer taxes on contributions to and potential earnings from a 401(k) plan until they take withdrawals. A traditional IRA is another tax-qualified retirement account many people use.

While you'll pay tax on most withdrawals from both retirement vehicles, Roth IRA owners enjoy tax-free earnings and withdrawals. The special tax provisions of a Roth IRA, to which you contribute after taxes, are unlike any other qualified retirement vehicle.

However, tax-qualified plans, as defined by the IRS, are not the only type of investment to offer tax advantages. The earnings inside annuities aren't taxed until withdrawal, and after-tax payments made to purchase them aren't taxed again when withdrawn. Tax-free bonds, like many municipal bonds, are just that—tax-free, at least on the federal level.

Other investments you might have through your broker or an online account are taxable, as is any income you might receive from a rental property. Social Security payments may be taxable or not, depending on your total annual taxable income. Some states also exempt Social Security payments and other retirement plan distributions from their tax reach.

This all matters because the tax treatment of your investment should determine when and how much to withdraw in retirement.

TAX DEFERRAL IS NOT THE END-ALL

However, taxes aren't the end-all to retirement income. Some experts believe the best thing to do with tax-deferred plans is to take distributions from them only after you spend down your taxable investments. The thinking is that tax deferral gives your investments more time to grow free without taxation. Then, you can take retirement distributions when you're older and your income is theoretically smaller—thus less taxes.

I don't believe in defer, defer, defer. I believe you'll need more money early in your retirement versus later, when you will likely be less active. Do you really want to make a bet that taxes won't be higher tomorrow, when you begin taking withdrawals from tax-deferred accounts, than they are today?

BECAUSE LIFE ISN'T COMPLICATED ENOUGH

The other huge factor that can upend a taxable investment-first strategy is something called required minimum distributions (RMD). Congress created tax-qualified investment vehicles to encourage Americans to save, but it doesn't want you or me to game the system by keeping tax deferral forever. So, the IRS created rules about when owners of tax-deferred accounts must take RMDs.

In IRS-speak, this means you must begin taking RMDs from a traditional IRA, 401(k) plan, and every other tax-qualified retirement vehicle other than a Roth IRA "for the year in which you turn age 70½. However, the first payment can be delayed until April 1 of the year following the year in which you turn 70½." Subsequent RMDs must occur by December 31 of each year.

Knowing this, why not opt for tax control instead of all tax deferral all the time? Take money out of your traditional IRA every year instead of waiting until age seventy and a half, when RMDs likely will be higher. Take from your other investments. The truth is you just don't know what your tax bracket will be at age seventy and a half. If you really don't need to spend your traditional IRA money, consider taking part of it each year and converting the amount to a Roth IRA. Remember that the Roth is tax-free.

ANNUITIES

Annuities are another investment some people buy for retirement. Just the word *annuity* triggers verbal warfare in the financial community, because of their heavy fees and expenses. There are three core types of annuities, and that is where the confusion begins.

Fixed deferred annuities are tax-deferred products that lock your funds up, typically for several years, for a fixed rate for an initial amount of time, typically one year. They are straightforward but lower-yielding products designed for people seeking to eliminate investment risk.

Variable annuities are also tax deferred but have a variety of investment options, like mutual funds, and come with countless pages of disclosures. Any product with this much fine print should make investors pause. Many advisors, me included, are certain a variable annuity's excessive charges drastically reduce its potential earning power. When a typical variable income annuity pays 2–3 percent, these fees can almost wipe out conservative investors' returns and take a huge bite out of potentially larger earnings of aggressive variable-annuity investors. I guess there is some comfort in knowing that you can also buy—at additional cost, of course—optional features called riders to protect your income stream.

An immediate annuity is another product you can buy to create a fixed income. Unlike a fixed annuity, which offers regular payments later, this annuity pays you immediately, as the name implies. Again, you give an insurance company a big check, and they promise you income for ten years, twenty years, or for life. Who buys this? People who want less risk, lower long-term investment costs, and the certainty of receiving income for the rest of their retirement.

Insurance agents who sell annuities obviously like annuities, which like them back in the form of commissions and other fees. Other agents are generally altruistic, believing that income annuities provide certainty in an uncertain financial world. Some retirees need this certainty.

I subscribe somewhat to this last group in limited circumstances, like when my clients are utterly risk averse and demand certainty. Remember what I said earlier? My clients with a little guaranteed income in retirement and no debt sleep the best.

As for variable annuities—forget it. I won't buy nor recommend this money trap, because their costs erode their rate of return. Moreover, insurance actuaries assume long life spans—longer than most of us will live—and add to the hidden costs with what's known as mortality charges.

So, if my client demands one, I'll search for an immediate fixed annuity with relatively small mortality charges, expense fees, and asset management rates. In this way, I can get my clients an extra percent or two above what they might get on a bank CD. But make no mistake about it, buying an annuity is the realization that you're trading money in for certainty the rest of your life. I use it only when it fits.

Quick Guide #19: What to Do about Social Security and Medicare...and When

From the time you bought your first car or home to when you began saving for retirement, you dealt with complexity that seems inherent in most financial products. Now, as you near retirement, you've navigated this obstacle course of complexity and want to start looking forward to a retirement of simplicity.

Not yet, ladies!

As you pass age sixty, you'll need to address how to take Social Security and Medicare. Both federal programs are must-haves for just about every retiree, but you probably will need help to make the right choices. The following information provides some of the basics for each program.

SOCIAL SECURITY

For many people, Social Security will comprise a significant portion of retirement income. Social Security benefits represented about 34 percent of the income of the elderly in 2016. The trick is for each individual to get the most out of this program.

First, decide when to begin taking payments. You can begin taking payments from the day you turn sixty-two up to when you turn seventy. The Social Security Administration uses what it calls your *full retirement age* to calculate how much it will pay you. Currently, people born between 1943 and 1954 have a normal retirement age of sixty-six. This age will rise gradually until those born in 1960 or after reach age sixty-seven.

The age when you take Social Security payments will affect monthly benefits for the rest of your life. Assume a person born in 1960 would earn a $2,000 monthly Social Security benefit at full retirement age. Now look at the difference between taking the benefit at sixty-two and at seventy:

1. **Begin payments at age sixty-two, and receive $1,400 per month, a 30 percent loss of benefits versus benefits beginning at full retirement age.**

2. **Begin payments at age sixty-seven—full retirement age—and receive $2,000 per month.**
3. **Begin payments upon turning age seventy, and receive almost $2,500 per month.**

As you can see, the difference between retiring early and delaying retirement dramatically changes your Social Security benefit. You can figure your own expected payment by visiting the Social Security Administration's retirement age calculator.

When to begin Social Security payments is an extremely personal decision. Your health, family longevity history, and other current situations will determine when you begin payments. Talk to your family and financial advisor to help you decide.

Married couples should also seek financial help to work out a formula that gets the most in Social Security benefits. If I could make a blanket suggestion, understanding that every situation is at least a little different, I would say the person with the smallest benefit should begin payments at sixty-two and the other spouse should delay until age seventy. Remember, the government will pay you 7–8 percent per year to delay payments.

Then I would recommend converting some of your taxable retirement account money to a Roth IRA, if you don't trigger a higher-than-expected federal tax bill.

SOCIAL SECURITY AND WORK

That's not the end of the rules. Continuing to work while receiving Social Security payments before your normal retirement age can be especially costly. If you are under full retirement age for the entire year, Social Security deducts one dollar from for every two dollars you earn above a certain limit. In the year you reach full retirement age, expect a one-dollar deduction for every three dollars you earn above the limit for that year, up until the month you reach your full retirement age. Once reaching full retirement age, these deductions stop.

The Internal Revenue Service won't tax benefits for lower-income retirees, subject to a <u>complicated formula</u> it explains on its website, and some states also exempt this income from taxes.

MEDICARE AND MORE

The other pillar of your retirement security revolves around Medicare and its alphabet soup components. Together, these parts help complete the puzzle that is health insurance once you reach the qualification age of sixty-five.

Medicare Part A is what used to be known as major medical. The government helps pay for inpatient hospital care and some skilled nursing facility costs after an eligible hospital stay. Most people who spent time in the workforce receive this insurance at no charge.

Medicare Part B pays for outpatient services, plus some medical equipment and preventive services. You pay for Part B—more if you exceed the income limit. You also pay a lifetime penalty of 10 percent per year for every year you don't register for this coverage once you are age-eligible, so pay attention to deadlines. Medicare Part D helps pay for prescription drug coverage, for which you pay a premium.

These Medicare plans offer high deductibles in some cases and co-payments in others. These can be especially costly, which is why many Americans also pay for Medigap insurance from private insurers. Medigap is supplemental insurance that pays for a portion of the costs not covered by Parts A, B, and D.

There are ten types of Medigap plans (they have letters, too) with varying degrees of coverage. Every plan with the same letter must offer the same level of benefits, but costs for Medigap plans within the same letter group can differ drastically by state and insurance company. Medicare's website at www.medicare.gov can help you compare costs and features of these plans.

Finally, if all this mix-and-match coverage is too much for you, explore Medicare Part C. Also known as Medicare Advantage, this is comprehensive health insurance coverage from private insurers approved by

Medicare. Part C takes the place of everything else I've described here except Part A.

WHEN TO ENROLL

There's a different way to sign up for Medicare seemingly for every situation, which doesn't make the process easy for some people. It is easy if you received Social Security retirement benefits before age sixty-five, because then you're automatically signed up for Parts A and B.

Everyone else has specific timeframes in which they must enroll or face lifetime late enrollment penalties. Generally, you must sign up for Medicare three months before to three months after turning sixty-five at www.socialsecurity.gov. However, when you continue to work for an employer with twenty or more employees or you're retired but covered by a spouse who gets coverage through a large employer, you don't need to sign up for Medicare until you lose the coverage. In this situation, employer coverage is the primary insurance, and Medicare, in which you can still enroll if you want, is the secondary payer.

If you or your spouse have employer-provided coverage through a company with fewer than twenty employers, sign up for Medicare Parts A and B, which becomes your primary coverage. Employer-provided health insurance becomes your secondary coverage.

If you receive retiree benefits from a former employer (or your spouse does and you are insured through your spouse's plan), the rules are different still. Sign up for Medicare by age sixty-five. It will become the primary insurance coverage at that age, with the retiree insurance becoming the secondary payer.

There's a lot more to know about Medicare, and the federal government has written a book about it. You can find much more information about Medicare and related issues on the Medicare website. Better yet, talk to a professional who understands the ins and outs of retiree health insurance.

Quick Guide 20: What Happens if You Run Out of Money? A Reverse Mortgage May Help

Sometimes even the best plans don't work the way you hope. Maybe you lost your job in your early or mid-fifties and didn't save what you hoped. Perhaps you ran into unexpected medical expenses or experienced other financial hardships.

You could continue to work, adding to your retirement kitty and delaying retirement account withdrawals. You could sell your home, assuming it has a lot of equity, rent, and then invest the rest, giving you something to live on in addition to Social Security benefits. And if you have a large cash-value life insurance policy and no beneficiaries, you might consider cashing it in. However, not everybody has these options. For these people, a reverse mortgage might provide at least a partial answer.

Reverse mortgages are for people who want to stay in their homes and have little to no liquid investments for retirement. You've seen the ads for them—typically touted by a good-looking, older actor. Although they are federally regulated, they're expensive, confusing, and have heavy fees.

Think of a reverse mortgage this way: As you paid your mortgage, the amount you owed decreased over time. Because this unique financial vehicle makes payments to you, it increases the amount of money you owe on the home—the reverse of what happened when you had a regular mortgage.

A reverse mortgage will guarantee how much total money you can expect to receive, and you can take the money in monthly payments or as a lump sum. Your mortgage may stipulate a lower monthly payment to you if interest rates rise, but it could increase payments if an appraisal shows your property has increased in value.

Before you take on this mortgage, you'll need to attend a credit counseling appointment, get a termite inspection, pay your property taxes, and keep the house maintained.

As a last resort, a reverse mortgage can provide a way to stay where you want to be—in your own home. Do your research, and ask a family member or advisor to help you analyze your choices. Go to the US Department of Housing and Urban Development's website to learn more.

Nine

Investing: It's All in Your Head

As we reach the end of this book, I hope you picked up something useful from *The Hardworking Woman's Guide to Money*. If only we could reach our individual financial end points just as easily.

The truth is that our goals evolve from the time we make our first financial decisions—or even before, if we paid attention to our parents' financial habits as I did—until we take our last breath.

You can learn successful financial habits, voraciously consume financial information, and earn advanced financial designations, like I have, and still have challenges to continually overcome. We are thinking, breathing human beings, and our psyches can jumble the plans of even the most prepared.

Although your head knows a few tricks as you attempt to avoid financial pitfalls, your heart can direct you to a place where you do not act in your own best financial interests. Parents know what I'm talking about.

How hard is it to say no to bankrolling your child's Ivy League education even when an almost equal alternative is half the price? Would you watch your daughter struggle to pay wedding costs she wasn't fully aware of, putting her reception in jeopardy? Or would you come to her rescue at the last minute to the detriment of your retirement savings?

I have clients and friends who have done both, knowing in the back of their minds that their actions would delay other goals. That's OK if you accept the consequences. When it comes to our children, we're only human. Psychology—and the deep desire to always provide our children with the very best—drowns out any other voice that might instruct us to take the more prudent financial approach.

The truth is people act against their own best interests in other areas of their financial lives all the time, from buying a home with more of mortgage than they can afford to charging a luxury vacation on credit cards with no plan to pay it back. In the investing world, some people invest—and I use this word lightly—in a way that doesn't keep pace with inflation. Others buy formerly hot stocks just as their flames flicker out, to the detriment of their investing goals.

Behaviors like these remind me of a saying I heard my mom repeat many times: "Every day, people act against their own best interests and do things they know they shouldn't."

Why do we do what we do, even when it isn't in our best interest?

UNDERSTAND YOUR INVESTING PSYCHE

Ultimately, you will make the financial decisions that best meet the needs of your family. I would never question the size of any parent's heart for helping a child financially. But other habits are hurtful in more than financial ways. There are millions of Americans who certainly know not to smoke, overeat, or text when driving.

And yet we do.

The pop psychologist in all of us has a way of compartmentalizing this risk. Smokers might believe they can stop whenever they want, so smoking won't hurt them. Couch potatoes might convince themselves that inactivity hurts others, not them. The mind is a fickle master.

TOOLS TO STEER US RIGHT

For many years, psychologists have explored why we continue to practice bad personal habits, but they have only begun tackling how and why we act against our own financial interests. Behavioral finance practitioners are working to determine why we make the financial decisions we do, both rational and irrational.

We invest too aggressively, as if trying to win the lottery.

We invest too conservatively, earning barely above 0 percent because we're so paralyzed with fear of losing principal, knowing that a meager return will reduce our spending power when you factor in inflation.

We ignore our investments when we need to monitor them to some degree so that obvious losers don't bring our investment portfolios' return down due to lack of oversight.

We tinker too much, racking up trading costs and other fees and charges that subtract from any investment return we might have.

And we don't spread our investments around—that's asset allocation—risking a sharp decline in an investment's value and consequently producing an outsized negative effect on our investments.

Before behavioral science became popular, Nobel Prize–winning economist Harry Markowitz recognized human nature when he created modern portfolio theory. This is the hallowed ground where I was educated, which basically says that investors act in their own best interest and respond to all known changes, knowing that reward requires some sort of risk.

By now, we know that investors do not always act in their best interests. Moreover, we can only know what we know—which will always be less than what someone else knows. Markowitz's work is most applicable to women investors when he says that reward requires some risk. Studies have proven time and again that women invest more conservatively than men. In many cases, that's a good thing. But when your investment strategy is too conservative to meet your goals that is a problem.

I would suspect Markowitz knew people are not robots. As fast as we live today, we remain creatures prone to the influences of the psyche. After all, how much will eating too many desserts really affect our weight? Can't we always work out harder tomorrow or eat less the following day? By now, we know this doesn't work. Making up for investing losses that didn't have to happen is equally difficult.

Markowitz writes about other things like correlation and variance and a whole world of technical investing theories I won't get into here. But one of his theories that is important to mention is about diversification, which is the idea of owning different types of investments to smooth out performance of investment returns. When you spread your risk around, you avoid the idea of having all of your assets in the worst investment of that year, but it also means you will not have all your money in the best one either. Smoothing investment return is most important for investors in the spending years, but it is also valuable for those who have acquired the majority of funds they will save.

I can poke a hole in a lot of investing advice you may have heard over the years. My favorite is when mutual fund companies urge you to sit and do nothing with your mutual fund investments. Now, there are a few reasons that trading mutual funds frequently is not a good investing idea. This doesn't, however, mean you should never trade a poorly performing mutual fund for another.

The only people who believe you should never move your money from one fund to another—or buy and hold—are the people paid by companies making money from the fees and charges they impose on your poorly invested money. They take advantage of investor inertia.

Some financial types have created tools that work with investors' bad habits to make them better. For those employees who might not contribute to a 401(k) plan due to inertia, some companies now automatically enroll them and generally put 3 percent of their salary into an appropriate investment choice.

Inertia also causes us to leave our 401(k) contributions and investments alone. Now there are tools that do the work for you when you need it. Contribution escalators increase the money you put into an employee retirement account when you receive raises. Automatic rebalancing is a staple that periodically adjusts the percentage mix of your investments in stocks, bonds, real estate, and money.

Nobel Prize winning Economist Richard Thaler, is the architect behind many of these investment tools and a concept called mental accounting, which is a way of describing how we segment our money decisions. We marvel at how much we save but don't think about how much we spent. When we invest, we rave about how much money we made on a stock but rarely count the dollars lost in a stock gone bad. When you add the pluses and minuses, would you have done just as well if neither happened?

Counting your wins but not your losses is human nature. We focus on the healthy lunch we ate and the walk we took after it but ignore the big meal and dessert waiting for us at dinner. We have all been there. We know that the best way to lose weight is to write down everything we eat. But who does that?

So, recognizing that we won't do *everything* we *know* we should do, why not use mental accounting for good instead of segmentation? Share a dessert with a dinner mate and learn that you saved two hundred calories you didn't eat.

Now imagine this. If you don't eat anything out of the ordinary and split this desert every day for six months, you will have passed on consuming 36,400 calories during this period. You can't help but lose weight with those numbers. Little steps equal big results, and we beat our psyches to boot. All this from doing a little mental accounting.

Why not use your ingrained habits to do mental accounting that helps you improve your investing skills, too? Consider the following examples:

- **Buy low, sell high.** I often say to clients, "You either like the price [buy low] or like the view [buy high] when it comes to investing." Typically, if a stock excites you, it has already increased in price significantly and is no longer cheap. I've been working with retail clients for twenty-five years, and the story never changes. People buy stocks when their prices are highest but avoid those stocks that drop and are less expensive. A little mental accounting can help you change this behavior.
- **Don't follow the herd.** Chalk up another bad money habit to the herd mentality. No one likes to be left behind, so when stocks rise and you know people made money, you say, "I want some of that." The higher the stock price soars, the more the herd piles on at the top. This is when the professional investor starts to trim. We all know what happens next. Prices fall, proving for the one

zillionth time that the market-timing thing is really hard. Leave the herd behind, and don't invest in anything when its price is at its highest.

- **Don't gamble.** Poker players hate when novices call them gamblers, insisting their game is one of skill, not chance. Investing is also a skill, but not one in which you can time what the market will do. Market timers have heard numerous warnings before, so they continue to attempt this near-impossible feat. This can be a very expensive habit. Investors who trade too much, double down on a poorly performing investment, or jump in and out of the market while watching the business news every day are bound to become poorer. They gamble, and we know gamblers almost always lose.

- **Don't trade too much.** You already know market timing doesn't work. When you trade too much, you also accumulate trading fee after trading fee. This can only make whatever winners you might have less profitable. Even without the fees, I've seen employees trying to time their purchases of mutual fund shares within a 401(k) plan. The problem is that mutual funds only trade at the close of the day at a price unknown until the next day, so this is fishing for profits while wearing a blindfold. It doesn't work.

- **Temper your confidence.** This leads to my personal favorite investing trait: overconfidence. There's an often-cited study that has made the rounds for years illustrating my point. About 75 percent of people think they are better than average drivers, but we know only 49 percent can prove this statistic. In my own unofficial survey, investors who ever earned a dime investing think they are better than the average investor. Again, only half are better than average.

- **Don't let inertia rule.** I don't like to generalize when I talk about women investors, but the truth is we do tend to be more conservative, more inert, and less confident. Sometimes we lose opportunities because of these behaviors. I've seen it. When the view is not good, women are more nervous, more cautious about investing.

One good habit women investors practice is a proclivity to do a little research or engage with someone who does it for them. Men are much more likely to exhibit overconfidence, often without cause.

TAKE CHARGE

So, my parting words?

Understand your investing psyche. Examine the money challenges keeping you up at night, and find the solutions—yourself or through a professional—that will let you sleep easier.

Understand why you spend and what you spend on. Understand you don't have to live a life of hardship to prepare for tomorrow.

Take advantage of automatic investment tools, from contributions to rebalancing.

Increase your retirement contributions until you reach the maximum allowed by your plan or account. Increasing your savings is a learned discipline and takes years to master, but don't get discouraged.

Don't give up. It's almost never too late to learn and invest in goals you hold dear. Money is only an instrument by which you can achieve other things. The choice is yours.

Epilogue

Count on Change—and More of the Same

Since I began writing this book, the world has been turned upside down by national elections here and abroad that challenge the status quo. Yet, as I write this chapter with summer dawning, status quo is what we continue to have.

A lot of noise from all sides, and little to no change.

Where does this leave us?

Thanks to technology, we can scream at each other and at our elected officials twenty-four hours a day via Facebook, Twitter, and countless other social media outlets. Thanks to this constant drumbeat, we worry about running out of money, losing our jobs, the stock market going down, our independence waning, and scores of other important and not-so-important things in life.

With so much noise, it's easy to feel like we have no control or influence. How can we plan when we don't know what taxes and healthcare in retirement will look like? Geez, it's hard to plan for next year—forget about ten years from now.

And yet we must.

What all this noise drives home is the importance of and need to plan financially for yourself and loved ones, because you never know which way government winds will blow. What we say, how we set ourselves up for the future, how we save and plan—these are all decisions we need to make for ourselves, because no one will do it for us.

If I could encourage you to do one thing, it would be to push away your fears and worries, the screamers and the naysayers, and make a plan for yourself—come hell or high water. Do this knowing that everybody has struggles, challenges, and bad days, so you're likely to encounter the occasional obstacle, too.

Take baby steps or choose a comprehensive plan, but lay the groundwork for a better financial tomorrow, because you are the architect, financier, and beneficiary of this planning.

And then, when you have all done all you can do to prepare financially for tomorrow, relax and ignore all the noise around you.

Because all you can do is all you can do.

Sources

AARP Public Policy Institute
United States Census Bureau
United States Department of Health and Human Services Centers for Disease Control and Prevention
Pew Research
MetLife Mature Market Institute
United States Department of Labor Bureau of Labor Statistics
New York Times
United States Department of Commerce
Washington University
Family Caregiver Alliance
Social Security Administration
Forbes
Wealth-X and NFP Family Wealth Transfers Report
The College Board
Federal Reserve Bank of New York
The Wall Street Journal
United States Department of Education
U.S. News & World Report
Kaiser Family Foundation
The American Institute of CPAs
Financial Industry Regulatory Authority

The Kaufmann Foundation
Internal Revenue Service
United States Centers for Medicare & Medicaid Services
U.S. Department of Housing and Urban Development

About Kathleen (KT) Thomas

Kathleen Thomas, who often goes by KT, has over 25 years of experience in the financial services industry and understands the need for women to take control of their financial lives.

A Certified Investment Management Analyst, CIMA®, Certified Financial Planner, CFP®, and Chartered Life Underwriter, CLU®, Thomas earned her degrees in Finance and Political Science from Salem State University.

Prior to founding NewDay Solutions, an Independent Registered Advisor Firm, Thomas spent 23 years as a Private Wealth Advisor for Ameriprise Financial Services. Many of her earliest clients continue to work with her.

Thomas is an avid long-distance runner and triathlon participant. She has completed the Boston Marathon seven times and the Ironman Distance Triathlon three times. She has volunteered as coach and mentored for Girls on the Run New Hampshire and Team in Training.

Raised in Massachusetts, Thomas now lives in Seabrook, New Hampshire, with her husband, John. They have one daughter, Jaclyn.

Made in the USA
Middletown, DE
31 January 2018